Alfred Henry Lloyd

Citizenship and Salvation or Greek and Jew

A Study in the Philosophy of History

Alfred Henry Lloyd

Citizenship and Salvation or Greek and Jew
A Study in the Philosophy of History

ISBN/EAN: 9783337070281

Printed in Europe, USA, Canada, Australia, Japan

Cover: Foto ©Lupo / pixelio.de

More available books at **www.hansebooks.com**

CITIZENSHIP AND SALVATION

OR

GREEK AND JEW

A Study in the Philosophy of History

BY

ALFRED H. LLOYD, Ph.D. (Harvard)
ASSISTANT PROFESSOR OF PHILOSOPHY IN THE UNIVERSITY
OF MICHIGAN

BOSTON
LITTLE, BROWN, AND COMPANY
1897

CONTENTS.

Part I.
THE DEATH OF SOCRATES.

Chapter	Pages
I. Greece	1–34
II. Rome	35–62

Part II.
THE DEATH OF CHRIST.

I. Judea	63–87
II. Rome Falls	88–114

Part III.
RESURRECTION.

The Christian State	115–142

CITIZENSHIP AND SALVATION.

Part I.

THE DEATH OF SOCRATES.

CHAPTER I.

GREECE.

I.

THE history of Greece is not as essential a part of education as it used to be. It is no longer thought to be indispensable to culture. In other ways than the way of Greece the rise and the fall of ideals and of the institutions embodying them are studied. Thus in the many biological sciences the same opportunity is found for observing the process of adjustment in all its details of life and death; and the same application to one's own life is possible, if not inevitable, in them. Not history, of whatever events, nor yet science, of whatever branch, but application to self is what makes for real culture, and at the present time the ideal in education seems to be to encourage such studies in any individual case as will insure application. So Greek life and thought, often found wanting as a means to culture, has now and again been supplanted by what have been thought to be more living or more practical themes. Practice and culture have refused to be divorced.

But, true as the decline of the study of an ancient civilization is, one must not be so narrow as to misunderstand it. Any particular study, whatever it be, is always set free when it ceases to be indispensable, and to the smaller number of those who still turn themselves to it the opportunities are increased and the rewards are unspeakably enhanced. Specialization, relegation to a few of any particular line, deepens and ennobles; it does not degrade; it brings into the activity all the increased power, all the exaltation, all the developed insight, that the very increase in number of ways to truth is evidence of. From the simple nature of the case, the special study cannot remain what it was when general; it must adjust itself to the richer experience of the community in which it has become special. If an adjustment from within fail, then that subtle form of adjustment from without, sometimes known as "translation," sometimes as "involution," will be forced upon it. The past is ever mortal; only the present can survive.

Accordingly in these chapters on the death of Socrates I would, so far as possible, fulfil the ideal which I have just defined for special study. I would, if possible, escape the specialism of those, who, though having eyes, refuse to see the living present day meaning of what is before them. I would be no mere antiquary and no hero-worshipper. I would neither exalt nor degrade paganism in any of its great achievements. I would simply illustrate as clearly and forcibly as I can a principle of life to-day. As a biologist, then, if I may assume an unearned title, I would go back to the days when Socrates, the great Greek philosopher, corrupter of youth, maligner of the Gods, public nuisance and offender against the laws, drank the fatal hemlock.

Socrates' life was a life of persistent advocacy of an idea, and in his death mankind has seen one of the grandest expressions of martyrdom ever accomplished in history. Again and again that death has been compared even with the sacrifice of Christ, and certainly no one refuses to admit some parallelism between the careers of the two men. There are those, however, who withdraw from any close scrutiny of the parallelism, and I must withdraw too, although for what at least on the surface will hardly seem to be the same reasons. History, as I conceive it, has such need of both characters and both martyrdoms that any attempt at comparison appears to me idle. I recall a sentence that was originally from Rousseau, but that came to me first through an elementary reader, before I had left the lower grades of the grammar school. Here it is: "Socrates died like a philosopher; but Jesus Christ, like a God." Now, my feeling at the time was that dying like a philosopher must be something altogether wicked. In my youthful acceptance of the rather attractive sentence, what with its striking antithesis and all, I felt sorry on the whole for Socrates, and probably the effect on me was exactly the reverse of what was intended. I wondered why anybody had ever gone to the trouble of drawing the contrast if the two cases were so unlike, and I have had ever since a keen interest in the life and death of Socrates. The objection to the contrast or comparison, moreover, that I vaguely felt then, I feel still, but of course more clearly and more positively. Rhetorical antitheses may stir the emotions, but often they are not quite honest. They do something that is not far from injustice; they cloud the truth. Certainly Socrates lived and died, and his death was a martyrdom, and the very idea for which above all others Christianity stands — the idea namely of the divinity of man — justifies one in saying that he achieved whatever is essential in the act of self-denial.

Mere comparisons or mere contrasts, therefore, aside, I am to look to Socrates and his times for some light upon the true nature of self-denial; I am to make a biological study of self-denial. Obviously the undertaking will involve a review of the events in the life of Greece long before Socrates' day, since without this only the most shallow appreciation of Socrates himself would be possible. And, furthermore, for the reason that every action, in particular every great action, is chiefly significant as the forerunner of a larger expression of itself in nature, or at least in the life immediately encompassing its original agent or prophet, the completest, the most richly suggestive manifestation of that for which Socrates stands in human experience will lie in the course of events following his death. I have, then, or rather we have, if any other has followed me so far, to consider, in the first place, the death of Socrates as the positive event at Athens, and, secondly, the death of Socrates, in a more abstract or a more spiritual sense, as fulfilled in the subsequent fate of Greece, when Greece was drawn into the Empire of Rome.

As for any cherished ideals let us recognize once for all that they must rather gain than lose through such a study as we are contemplating;

and if in the end a truly living appreciation of the other sacrifice achieved at Jerusalem is made possible, the present labor will have returned something that must far exceed in its practical worth the temporary satisfaction of any partisan comparison.

II.

THE history of Greece shows a race living through two very different fears. Thus there came first to Greece the fear of annihilation from without, and, secondly, the fear of annihilation from within. A life with these two fears, moreover, is typical. Individuals, men as well as nations, experience no other. But the case of Greece is striking.

As to the first fear of Greece, the early Greek civilization, scattered as it was in independent communities through the coast countries of Asia Minor, the islands of the Ægean, and the mountain-bound districts of Greece proper, fell into great danger, not only of attack, but even of conquest from the East and from the South; and the danger as it grew brought about centralization, making necessary the unification of a hitherto dismembered people. It created in each part a demand for men of something more than mere military sagacity. "Wise men" became the rivals of generals. Philosophy, statesmanship, legislation, rose into prominence. The idea of a national capital came to each of the separate communities. And, although in the earlier thoughts of unity no one ever even dreamed of centralization at Athens, still a single capital of all Greece was inevitable in course of time; for an idea, once afield, is sure to break from its assigned bounds.

But the movement in Greek history towards centralization at Athens had another side. No fear is without its hope. No necessity is without its opportunity. In short, from within as well as from without came the demand for unification, the outer stimulus in this case, as in all cases, only answering to an inner motive. That threatened conflict with the barbarians was surely no result of wholly external events, for the Greek only brought it upon himself; his evolution required it; and the device of a national capital was not for mere self-defence, but was the necessary outcome of self-expression. Thus, at the very moment when the danger from without befell them, the Greek communities had become conspicuous for their prosperity, independence, and aggressiveness or outwardly reaching activity; and their prosperity and activity, accompanied as it naturally was by the rise of a leisured class and the delegation of the more commonplace labors to servants or slaves, led to conscious reflection. Society became divided, and if division under such conditions implies anything of signal importance, whether in a society's or in an individual's activity, it implies the consciousness of unity as an ideal. Not only, therefore, does it make a reflective consciousness possible, but also it determines the idea upon which the consciousness will feed. Indeed, unity must be the ideal to all thinking, to all consciousness; and in practice this means that a division, that is to say, a differentiation or delegation of functions within the life of a community, by giving rise to a thinking class and so bringing the people to a consciousness of itself and a sense of the need of unity, will disclose also a division or differentiation setting in on a much larger scale and including in its movement all other communities of like origin in religion and general racial experience. The single differentiated whole will always find itself but a part in an inclusive whole, and its desired unity within can be secured only through an adjustment without. The Milesian, for example, will recall as never before that he is also a Greek; brought to the point of saying, in the words of one of his wise men, that all things are water, his city being so nearly an island, his life and prosperity depending so much upon the waters surrounding him, and his gods themselves being born of the sea, he will at once perceive that the unity of all things can be expressed in terms of *any* one of them all, that unity is something deeper and greater than any particular element or than any particular city.

So, to repeat briefly, an inner prosperity, a laboring class, a leisured class, and a reflective consciousness are all inseparable phases of a people's life, and in them or in their very inseparableness we can see how, as has been said, the stimulus to unity and centralization which came through the danger of attack from without corresponded to a motive already realized within. The external stimulus had its internal sanction. Else how could response, reaction, the centralization itself, ever have taken place? No more in history than in one's own self-consciousness, than in the feeling about one's own activity, is it necessary to be deterministic.

Well, the danger without and the prosperity within, the one circumstance as much as the other, led to the unification of Greece. But the centripetal movement was not without what we have to see as its natural or logical counterpart, — a centrifugal movement. If the danger and the prosperity, as two inseparable aspects of the one movement in the development of Greece, were the promise of Athens, they were responsible also for the Greek colonies that sprang up along the entire Mediterranean coast, and particularly in Italy at the west. The danger made the transplanting wise, if not necessary, while the prosperity made it possible. Colonization, moreover, as a centrifugal movement, illustrates just what we saw a moment ago. It shows how unity, as an ideal determined by conditions at home, always brings positive relations to the larger sphere of life without. A people's sense of unity makes breaking away from the endangered dwelling place no altogether hopeless change. The world has become one essentially, and the people, having risen to an independence of its conditions, can settle anywhere and still be itself, and its gods, become equally free, can go with it.

Do but pause here, and in order to reflect a moment upon it review in your mind so much of the general history of Greece as we can now see. Thus, in its earlier stages the process that looked to the glory and supremacy of Athens is marked (1) by the rise in the separate communities of thinkers, "wise men," law-makers, whose chief interest, of course, is in bringing to light for themselves and their peoples the unity that underlies difference; (2) by threats and even attacks from barbarian peoples, in which the sense of difference and the end of unity must be greatly quickened; (3) by widening class distinctions within, calculated only to intensify the end by making it also a natural self-determined impulse; and (4) by resort both in self-defence and for more perfect self-expression to extensive colonization, in which above all else is asserted or enacted the principle that all the different parts of the world are essentially one, that mankind, whatever its original ties, can be itself anywhere. And in these marks of the process we have plainly no mere group of more or less isolated facts, we have rather a wonderfully beautiful whole; a fear that is one with a hope, a disintegration that is but incident to organization, and a wandering off to strange lands that is possible only under the same assumption that is the basis of centralization, Greek influence being spread far beyond the places of its childhood just in proportion as it is intensified and focused. A wonderfully beautiful whole, I say; a whole that lives, as we know life in our own times; a whole in whose life one can see, if one does but really look, a motive or a spirit struggling to free itself; and a whole, finally, whose motive or spirit, when one follows it to its fulfilment, shows the Athenian Socrates, fulfilment of the focusing or centripetal movement, and pagan imperial Rome, fulfilment of the spreading or centrifugal movement, and the two as inseparable as we have found Athens and the Greek colonies.

But we must return to the course of Greek history itself; we must, however rapidly, follow the struggle from the point at which we left it. So, — and I begin by making the long story very short, — the sense of unity in the world, whether as expressed in wars and migrations and political changes, or as packed concisely in a philosophical formula, has to lead to a sense of the unity of the individual self; the outer unity reveals to each single person an inner unity; cosmology, as in general the science of life without, evolves into psychology, the science of life within; and to the rule here indicated the progress of Greece was no exception. As said already more than once, the external stimulus corresponded to an internal motive. The motive, however, had to be in the single individual, if it was in the social whole. But fully to comprehend the sense of the unity of the individual self that came to Greece, we must consider the second great fear through which Greek civilization passed, the fear of annihilation, not from the barbarians — they were repulsed, but from the Greeks themselves.

III.

WITH the second fear what was all but apparent in the first is brought into clear light,—this, namely, that a people's conflict is never really with another people, but rather with itself; that the basis of an outer danger is always an inner danger.

Thus Marathon and Salamis and Plataea were all that was needed to show to Greece, centred at Athens, where her true danger lay. Nothing so surely as victory, even at the moment of exultation, will disclose where the still unconquered enemy lies. After winning so signally her great battles Athens soon discovered that the real battle had but just begun; that her real assailant, only disguised in the armies of the East, was a something, a national temptation perhaps, an impulse surviving in her nature from the time when the Greek race, as shown by its religion, language, and institutions, had been one in life and character and habitation with the very peoples that came against her. She discovered that realization of her innermost ideal or complete expression of her motive to unity, which the coming of Xerxes and the others only awakened, could never be merely through an heroic repulse, grand as that was, in a mountain pass, nor through putting to rout a host of ships. Such struggles and such victories only postponed the final struggle, although in the control that they required, in the respect for principle that they developed, they served to prepare the people for the real contest, compared with which to the historian in later days Thermopylæ and Salamis would seem but child's play.

Those victories begat conceit, self-consciousness, self-glorification. The conscious reflection previously turned to problems of civil administration and foreign policy, found a more attractive field in history, in dramatic poetry, and in architecture and sculpture and painting. Recall the Athens of the days of Pericles, if you would understand this. No sooner did Athens become the centre of Greece than she began to erect wonderful monuments of all kinds to her achievements.

But in the art and literature of Greece it is wrong to see a people only paying tribute to its past. Art always defines the past, and definition of the past sets the future free. The æsthetic consciousness, then, on which the fine arts depend, is quite as much a promise as a reminiscence; it comes at a moment of poise between the past and the future, between an acquired freedom and the use or application of it, between free but aimless action and duty; it shows duty for a time in abeyance. In Greek art, accordingly, there was more than a golden age, there was the closing in of the people's conflict. The expression of experience in works of art did for a time make the pulse beat faster with pleasure and sense of worth and power; but in the end the effect of putting the time-honored ways and long-cherished ideals and noble deeds and heroes upon the stage — for art in all its forms does just that — was to show where the battle was yet to be fought, in that it heralded an age of rationalism as successor to morality and piety and patriotism. Staging life, however reverently at first, had to lead in time to moral laxity, impiety, corruption in political life, and general social disintegration. It robbed life of all that had given it worth and coherence and power to satisfy the moral and religious natures; it made the traditional meaning of life external; it turned life into a form or convention, instead of a content with any substantial spiritual worth; into a something merely to be used, a something to which to adjust one's self, rather than what it had been, — an inner strength and support.

In the Greek plays, not to mention other indications of the change, natural law, rather as hard necessity than as realized opportunity, came to succeed the gods in the control of human life; and in order to appreciate the influence of these plays one must remember, first, that the principal theatre seated thirty thousand, those who were unable to afford the admission fee being admitted at the expense of the city; and, secondly, that hard necessity, fate, as the moral law, is quite alien and discouraging to any sense of moral responsibility. So, if the earlier effect of Greek art was æsthetic exhilaration, the later was to make sacred things secular, and, as has been said, to introduce a time of emphasis on mere utility and general indifference to anything but a most conventional morality. The Greek, by his art set outside of himself and so exposed to his own scrutiny, became in himself, as under the same conditions you or I would become, a mere atom, an element with no quality but that of number or price; and Greek society, from being the patriotic democracy that Pericles had imagined, degenerated into a mass of warring members or a composition of individuals who lived with each other on sufferance. In a word, the Greek found himself arrayed in a thoughtless, conscienceless, godless host against himself: his own enemy, his own danger, his own despair.

So the Greek in struggle with himself, not with himself disguised in a barbarian horde, as if an unrecognized but actual and materialized memory of himself, but with himself face to face, is the Greek of the second fear; and, if one may give perhaps a new turn to a familiar line, in order to make the picture as vivid as possible, " When Greek meets Greek, then comes a tug-of-war." At such a time neither colonization of any ordinary sort, with its wandering off to safer places, nor masterly generalship, can insure the continuance of a people's autonomy.

The second fear was sharper than the first, so sharp indeed that the senses seem to have been dulled to it, and naturally enough, since the danger of destruction was so great. But the second fear, like the first, was not without its hope; the stimulus to unity was not without the motive. Was not the second struggle a repetition of the first, although at very much closer quarters? The struggle had not changed; it had merely become personal, self-consciousness having succeeded patriotism; only the scene of action had changed. And yet to show the hope or the motive in the Greek's fear is not so easy now as it was before. In the later Greece, at least to one's first view, there appears only the stimulus, only a wholly external interest, in the concerns of life. The Greek, it is true, was brave in the presence of his great danger, and bravery is born of hope and will; but his bravery was of the sort that hides itself, he was brave to the point of bravado; he turned his back on his new danger.

Thus, in friendship founded upon utility; in politics plied as a trade through bribery; in fashion prevailing over duty; in blind fate as the only moral law; in a philosophy scouting all but the truth of the senses and teaching only rhetoric and oratory and the other forms of a wholly time-serving wisdom; in the Greek person, man or woman, become only a commodity on the market; in the Athens of Alcibiades and the Sicilian expedition, of the mutilation of the Hermes, of the Sophists, and of the Spartans as foes, instead of, as hitherto, rivals, seeking alliance with Persia,—in such a Greece, in such times, it is hard to see any positive interest in unity, any personal motive to it. But the interest and therefore the motive were there; concealed, perhaps, but real; unborn, but alive, and at least vaguely felt. Even bravado is not unconscious. Social relations on sufferance are still social.

The effort of a society to preserve its wholeness when its members avow and to all appearances practise nothing but individual isolation, is not without suggestion of pathos. There is so much contradiction in it, so much human perversity. But, after all is said, contradiction and perversity are the forerunners of progress. In what way, however, to show this in the special case before us I have found it hard to determine, but for my own thinking no evidence has been so striking as that of the standpoint of the mathematicians belonging to the same period. Thus, if the people in general were trying to keep up a social life, that is, to continue the movement that expression of social relations involves, in a society whose parts were regarded as wholly unrelated members or social atoms, and could discover no foundation for such a life but an empty conventionality, the mathematicians and logicians among them, breathing of course the same atmosphere, were trying to find motion in a space composed of absolutely portionless parts or mere points, and could only conclude that motion had no reality save that of an illusion of the senses. And, as regards their denial of reality to motion, I venture to say that with their standpoint you would reach the same conclusion. Certainly a space *filled* only with pure points, which are of course nothing but positions, must be a space in which distance is of absolutely no importance, and motion is hardly possible without distance. Thus, however many portionless parts, or points, you mass into a continuous whole, you will never get a space so composed that motion from any one to any other part will be at all significant. In such a space motion is literally rest. In such a space motion must be either all at once, an infinite number of positions being traversed instantaneously, or not at all, an eternity being required for an infinitesimal distance. In such a space "the flying arrow rests" and "Achilles, swift of foot, can never overtake the tortoise." The Greek, then, was right so far as he went, but he did not go far enough. Motion in a merely composite space *is* an illusion, just as social life in a merely composite community *is* the purest convention; but neither the portionless part, the point, nor the social atom, the Greek as a commodity with a price, has anything to do with mere composition. Both are positions or centres of relation, so that hidden within the very arguments, on which the denials of motion and of social life were founded, there was an idea which was to give science on the one hand and practical life on the other such an impulse as had never been known before. The idea was simply this, — that reality in any of its phases is not composite but relational or organic.

The Greek Sophists, accordingly, were in reality using terms that were much in advance of their understanding. They were building better than they knew. They were helping the future in spite of themselves. "Man is the measure of all things," they said, and imagined that so they made him a social atom, living in and for the moment. In so many words they declared that, as the flying arrow rests, so the social being, in spite of his social life, is only an isolated individual. A society of individuals as " measures," however, like a space of points as positions or relations, is no atomic agglomeration, but a whole whose life expresses law or system. Its different parts are parts only in name, since in it a universal selfhood that knows no parts is brought to the hour of its birth. Are the individual members of a society only "measures"? Then is the society itself a mechanism, and a mechanism presupposes a mechanic.

Accordingly, as said above, among the Greeks of selfishness and a conventional morality there was present and active the motive to unity; unborn perhaps, but alive and at least vaguely felt. The danger was not hopeless; the bravado was not vain.

IV.

Now what is birth? It is certainly no creation of something out of nothing. It is the timely formation and appearance, the embodiment and the setting free of an organized force, of an ideal vitally real and active from the beginning, or let us say of a motive which stimulus from without has quickened into fulfilment and individuation of itself. If, then, you look for the unborn motive in the Greece of the second period, you will find it, as but just now indicated, in the very cause and conditions of the fear. Fate and fashion and bribery and sensualism and unbelief, the natural incidents of atomism in society, are the motive all but realized. They are the pain before the birth. They show Greece in mortal conflict with herself. They show resistance before achievement.

Did it ever occur to you that the idea of fate can never be anything but a superstition or a time-server's excuse? Fate is no blind man's idea, but the idea of one who refuses to see his own fuller opportunity. Thus to talk about it at all is really to use it, and to use it at all is to deny it as fate. The Greek public, however, in one way and another was talking about it and using it. For them, then, as for all, it was a suppression of conscience, a sop thrown to duty. When, therefore, we see them given over to fashion and materialism and fatalism, we have to struggle hard with ourselves against something very much like a belief in spirits, so real seems the working of some spirit among them; and real only the more for their refusal to recognize it. As shadows tell of a light, so even bribery, obviously one result of fatalism, is evidence of a self that does not live for money; and disbelief, of belief; and the real of the moment, of that which is real always. We cannot, then, hear the Sophists at Athens proclaiming the too welcome doctrine of selfishness that " truth is nothing in itself, but man is the measure of all things, whether of their existence when they do exist or of their non-existence when they do not," without hearing from somewhere, from some one, whom we may not see at first, the illusion springing from our need of explaining the hollow sound in the Sophists' words, without hearing that " in the conviction of ignorance is the beginning of wisdom," that "he is the wisest who knows that his wisdom is in truth worth nothing." I say that we have to struggle with ourselves against the belief in spirits or something very much like it; but fortunately the course of history, as if true to the conditions of birth, supplemented the manifestation of an unbelieving people with a living personal witness to the hidden motive and the suppressed conscience. The spirit, whose voice we have seemed to hear, was no spirit; it was Socrates, commonly spoken of as the Father of Philosophy, but at least with as much meaning the son.

Vitally present in the life of Greece from the beginning, the very light that cast the shadows of the later Athenian life, Socrates came in person at just the moment when the time for fulfilment seemed darkest, when the shadows were longest and deepest. Ahead of his times, some have said, but that surely is only a petty conceit. As a motive in Greek life, always active and felt, he was always ahead of his times, even before he was born. He whom the times demanded, implied, contained, was hardly premature. He was in struggle with his times. He, too, heard the voice, or spirit, that we have heard. He was the inner motive of Greece that had in spite of all determined her destiny from the beginning, and that at the evening of her career appeared with the assurance that the conflict was not lost, but that in the very moment of greatest despair there was opportunity for further and still completer self-expression.

Yes, it seems as if we must have believed in Socrates had he never been born, so real is he in the history of Greek life; but of course he had to be born, so necessary is our belief in him; so impossible is the Greek, become a commodity on the market, a measure, a social atom, without him; so all but actual is he in Athens even before he lives to walk her streets and cross-question her unthinking people; so completely does a mechanical social life involve a living mechanic.

Socrates was himself a Sophist, a true citizen of his day, but far more so than any other. He faced the teaching and the life of his times directly. He took what he heard literally. He allowed no temporizing with himself or his experience. In his "I know that I do not know" at one stroke he refuted his less candid fellows out of their own mouths. Such refutation was irony of fate indeed, but it is the only real refutation. In his "Know thyself," he showed that the very atomism in society, the selfishness and the utilitarianism and the venality, was evidence of a higher nature in man; that man, the measure of all things, not in his individual sensuous selfhood, but in his universal selfhood, was a living reality. Living for the moment, he said in so many words, is nevertheless living for all time. "What is justice?" he asked, and somebody answered: "Dealing squarely with one's friends," or "Depriving an insane man of his sword," or "Not bullying the weak;" but, said Socrates: "Justice is surely no one of these things; justice is simply justice; friends or enemies or crazy men or weaklings have nothing to do with it. Know thyself as just essentially, not as just in this or that moment or under these or those conditions."

V.

So we have Socrates, without whom Greece had not been Greece. His birth was necessary, because he was the embodiment of an ideal that lay at the very heart of Greek life. But his death was necessary also.

History was not less logical than Socrates' own thought, and the Socratic thought itself amounted to a decree that its Athenian thinker should die, and die, too, as the result of his people's resentment. The death of Socrates and the manner of it were as necessary as his birth. You do not understand? But had not this remarkable Greek declared that justice had nothing to do with friends or enemies, with conditions here and now? Had he not said in plainest terms that the just man had no need of being an Athenian? What more natural, then, than that his fellows should take him as literally as he had taken them? History is always literal, and often grimly so.

But Socrates' relation to his times, his conflict with them, may be recounted in the following way. The notion of the person as a law unto himself or as an end unto himself as means is a common one. The self as end is of course the soul; as means, the body; so that the person as having both soul and body is an end unto himself as means. But Athens, with her social atoms, had at her disposal the self as means, and her social atomism only shows her become a miser in that she insists on taking the means for the end. Her Greek was become a commodity, or so much material wealth, which she might spend, if she would, but like others in the possession of new wealth she hoarded the means instead of using it. She was persistently blind to the fact that the means presupposed an end already determined, an ideal already real. The glitter and the ring of the sensuous life that her successes had put into her hands, held her spell-bound. And so Socrates found her. Yet he did not, as at first thought might be expected, break the spell. To be sure, he urged upon his people a recognition of the self as end; he bade them live no longer for the many, but for the one; he reminded them of the contradiction and the stultification in such a miserly life as theirs was; above the composite and momentary he set the indivisible and indestructible; but it takes more than mere negations to break spells.

Socrates did not break the spell that bound Athens, because as a matter of fact it bound him too. As I have said so many times, he was himself in the struggle of Greece, an integral part of it. He shared in the contradiction from which the times, whose atmosphere he breathed, could not be free. If you hold your right hand before a mirror, the reflection is rather of a left hand than of a right, the image being symmetrical with the object, not similar to it. In much the same way, then, Socrates and his life and teachings were symmetrical with the life and teachings of the

Athenian people whom he offended. He only reproduced, as if by a mirror's reflection, the contradiction which they were manifesting; he reproduced it, but the other way around. Thus, if they were misers, taking means for end, he was a spendthrift, a reformer, equally impractical, taking end for means. He and they, in short, were at one and yet in conflict; at one, because belonging to the same times, and in conflict, because the times were in conflict with themselves. The miser and the spendthrift are ever the most natural contemporaries.

In terms somewhat less technical the worldly life, which is a hoarding of the means, and the life apart from the world, which assumes that the end will realize itself, naturally go hand in hand. They complement and correct each other, and it is hard to say which of them is the more serious departure from duty, the worldliness or the abstract spirituality; but certainly both keep fulfilment in abeyance. Imagine a lot of boys in a carpenter's workshop. You know exactly what time-servers they will be; how they will use the things nearest at hand; and how their relations to each other will be maintained rather through sufferance than through any sense of co-operation in their activities. They will call themselves carpenters, but they will care more for the seeming than the being such. At last, however, as in time must happen, some one will turn upon them and exclaim: " Cutting boards or driving nails is not carpentry; nor is chiselling, nor sawing, nor planing; carpentry is carpentry; the one, not the many. You have called yourselves carpenters long enough. Now I am no carpenter, and I know that I am not. Do you also dismiss your conceits and know yourselves." Of course that is some young Socrates among them, and what will be the effect of his speech? Will the workshop, albeit well supplied with tools and materials, be any more productive than it was before? Hardly, or at least not at once. Carpentry in the abstract is no more productive than the boys' cutting and hammering and planing. The first effect of such a specch must be a demand from the group that the speaker, so wholly out of sympathy with life as he finds it, be put out of the way. Certainly that is what happened at Athens. Taking the end for the means, denying the means, brought quick retribution. The misers had no use for the reformer.

And in still another way, besides the symmetrical reflection of the confusion of end with means, we can see how Socrates both in his life and in his death belonged most vitally to his times. Thus he was as active and busy and self-assertive as any Greek in Athens. He was no abstract thinker; he organized no special school; his philosophy went on two legs and was known in every corner of Athens. Merchants and politicians and laboring men and great artists knew him, and had experience of the peculiar trade that he plied. For Socrates philosophy was no theory, but as direct and concrete an activity as any to be found in the city. Simply he met like with like. He went about from place to place, a self-seeker among self-seekers, bent on finding himself, or the motive and conscience of which he was the embodiment, and on making the active presence of these felt in the life of every one with whom he spoke. No man ever used others for his own self-realization so thoroughly as did Socrates. Savages use each others' fingers and toes as basis of numerical reckoning, abstract calculation being impossible to their untutored minds; but Socrates, turning the utilitarianism of his day completely back upon itself, used all Athens for the development of his thought. He fulfilled himself in the very life from which we have seen him to have sprung. He made others, in spite of themselves, see themselves, a suggestion of their duty, a hint of their artificiality, in him. Even his death was his use of them.

So I said above that the execution of Socrates

was as necessary as the birth, and this is becoming ever more apparent as our thought advances. Indeed, the sum of it all is that Socrates condemned and executed himself. We can conclude nothing else. Whether we say that his times took him literally when he declared justice to be simply justice, or that he exalted the end wholly at the expense of the means, thereby realizing such isolation of himself in Athens as no other Athenian, however much imbued with the individualism of the time, had ever accomplished, or that by his personal efforts throughout the city he made the people hate themselves and so most naturally condemn themselves in him, — from whichever side we approach the matter, Socrates stands out as his own destroyer. But, you remind me, he was brought to trial. That is true. Certain forms were complied with. Yet, aside from the fact that every reformer brought to trial is proved a reformer only if condemned, since the law which determines justice at court relies altogether on precedent, — aside from this fact, the defence of Socrates before his judges was but a short yet telling repetition of the career for which he had been brought to trial, so that the judges had no choice but to feel that out of his own mouth he had condemned himself. Moreover, the Socrates, as a condemning conscience, already awake within themselves, made them all the readier to accept the fatal evidence of the defence. Those, in general, who have been made to feel their own conviction of error are not disposed to make a careful discrimination in the case of another among them. Indeed, so vitally organic is the life of a society, condemnation of another is but self-condemnation. In other words, the presence of the motive in Greek life, which had made the birth of Socrates not possible, but necessary, was just that which through its birth in the conscious experience of the people made his execution inevitable. So, once more, without any effort at mere subtlety, literally, Socrates executed Socrates.

VI.

But this was to be a study of self-denial. Where now is the self-denial? So far we have found nothing of the kind. In the martyrdom of Socrates we have found only self-expression. Had the execution been unjust, had Socrates and his teaching been no inner motive of the life and times in which he found himself, had he been a mere harmless spectator in some hidden part of the city, had he taken no part in the Greek's struggle with Greek, in no way sharing in the contradiction of the day, had he been simply the Socrates that so much history and so much shallow sentiment have been fond of telling us all about, a man quite alone at Athens, literally ahead of his times, unappreciated, unreal, alien, even miraculous, then we might talk of self-denial. But the living Socrates of Greece's second fear, whether we see him at his trade, an artisan among artisans in the streets and by-ways of the city, or at his trial, or in the prison-cell with the cup of poison upon his lips, the living Socrates never denied himself. He ever showed exactly what he was. The self that he expressed, was, and was living and active and upon this earth before Athens sacrificed him or before he, as some would have it, denied himself. In a word, his death did not bring him into new life. It only proved his old life.

But, says somebody, no one has ever meant anything else by self-denial than just such self-expression. On the contrary, I think, as I have already hinted, that self-denial has often, if not usually, meant some unnatural thing, something requisite to secure the freedom of an unnatural in the sense of a supernatural selfhood; that is to say, self-denial has been regarded as a way to a remote not yet realized life, a sort of tool useful to an as yet unsaved and unfulfilled self. But what an impractical and unspiritual sentiment! As if a selfhood worth saving for eternity were not already secure, and not only secure but also active. True, self-denial is not without significance as a means to an end, but the end in its case, as in all cases, is real before, not merely after the use of the means; it is an active motive within so soon as it is a goal without. Thus the life and death of Socrates have shown to us the spiritual Socrates alive before the execution; nay, even before the birth. Socrates was born with his true self already real and active, so that perfectly direct expression, not salvation through self-denial, was his first duty, and he proved himself worthy of the responsibility.

In the next chapter we shall see how the true and spiritual self of Socrates continued to live after as it had lived before the life at Athens, and how on a larger scale, among nations rather than within a single people, the life and death of Socrates were repeated. And then, if possible, even more positively than now, self-denial will prove to be the way to the expression of an already active life, of an already living ideal.

CHAPTER II.

ROME.

I.

IT will be remembered that in an earlier paragraph of the former chapter the statement was made that every act, in particular every great act, is chiefly significant as the forerunner of a larger expression of itself in nature or at least in the life that immediately encompasses its original agent or prophet. Whatever an individual agent does, this means, sooner or later becomes or tends to become the action of a group large or small. Examples of this are plentiful, but it is perhaps most obvious in industrial division of labor, where an activity originally confined to one becomes the differentially shared activity of a number. Division of labor or functions, however, is not confined to industry in the narrow sense; it is a law of all adjustments, of all organic evolution. Just why, furthermore, the social repetition of an individual's act takes place is not hard to see, since, as we have discovered so positively in the case of Socrates, the original act is not the result of the expression of an impulse belonging solely to the individual; it comes from an impulse shared by him with all, so that his expression cannot but stimulate a repetition by the group to which he belongs. The group first acted in him, then he in them; he is but a leader, a prophet, one who has revealed to his fellows the necessities or opportunities of their nature; and not only does his act call out a reassertion of itself by him as in them, but also the reassertion is single, not multiple, since he has shown to them a nature that they have in common and that they must therefore express together. He makes them act as one.

Especially, it was said, is this social repetition true of great acts; and this, because greatness consists in the degree with which an impulse existing in society, a motive, dormant perhaps but real in the community, is brought into expression by an individual. Socrates in his death *fulfilled* such an impulse, and just for this reason was his death, or rather his action, the natural forerunner of the same action on the part of his race. His death was their doom; no, not their doom, but, by as much as Socrates himself realized a higher ideal of life, their hope and opportunity. In other words, the death of Greece is not to be looked upon as due merely to the Roman conquest, which approached fulfilment as Athens declined; it was equally the outcome of a motive in Greek life; it was inner self-expression, not self-denial; and the real agent in the process was not less Socrates as surviving in the life of his people than Rome. Hints have already forced themselves upon us that Socrates was but a Greek forestalling Rome.

If I say that Socrates lived as an active selfhood after his execution I am sure to be misunderstood in many ways. But that is just exactly what I have to say. He lived after his death, even as truly as he had lived before his birth. Indeed, in so far as we can understand his death only as self-expression, what conclusion is possible but this of his after life? By his after life, however, we can here refer to no spiritual, unworldly existence, nor can we mean, as some might imagine from a too literal acceptance of the words, existence on earth as some ghostly agent. The meaning here is far more practical, if not also far more inspiring to religious feeling. The very last thing intended is advocacy of spiritualism of any kind. Socrates' after life is in the activity, it is literally the activity of the Greek people carrying their struggle with themselves to its inevitable end in the supremacy of Rome, which, be it repeated, was as much their victory as Rome's. Socrates survived his death as the same selfhood which he had brought to so perfect an expression, the selfhood that before his birth had been the innermost motive of Greece, and that after his execution became her own freed activity. So the death of Socrates, in the second manifestation of it which we are to study, in its repetition in the death of his people, means fulfilment also; denial of Greece, perhaps, and of Greek institutions, but certainly not self-denial of the deeper Greek character, rather its more perfect self-expression in the rise of Rome.

II.

WE need here to define still more clearly, or more concretely, just in what the greatness of Socrates and the value of his achievements consisted. It does not seem quite enough to say after the manner of rather abstruse thought, that in him the Greek at last overcame himself. More in detail, Socrates achieved a victory over that besetting sin of Greek life, in the later as well as in the earlier times, which historians never fail to dwell upon but often fail to appreciate, namely, the inability to act in unison. Such inability was shown first in the petty jealousies of the different peoples during the foreign wars, and secondly in the subsequent individualism at Athens; but what the historians have often overlooked is that this sin, yes, this besetting sin, springing no doubt among other things from the geographical characteristics of the country, was not "original," but presupposed a co-existing motive to something better. Had the sin been "original," there could hardly have been any struggle; resistance to Persia would not merely have been idle but altogether unnatural; the different ways in which the Greeks met Persia, the centralization and the colonization would have been impossible movements in history; Socrates himself would have been a Persian slave, and happier so, instead of the Greek prophet that he was. And from the other side, if the Greek peoples had acted in perfect unison, if their jealousies had been quite absent, if the motive for union had been perfectly free, with no sin to make a conflict, the approach of barbarian Persia, supposing that it could ever have taken place, would not have suggested to Greece even the shadow of a danger, and there had been no Athens, no Greek art, and none of that independence of spirit that carried the Greeks to so many remote parts of the Mediterranean; there had been simply a Greek empire, in which life had been as thoroughly at a level as was ever realized in any oriental dynasty you might name. Greece's besetting sin was as much the salvation of the Greek as his destruction; her mountain ranges, her peninsulas, and her islands, were limitations that developed into freedom and worldwide opportunity, not of oriental existence, but of occidental action.

Over Greece's besetting sin of inability to act in unison Socrates achieved a signal victory. But we have seen that the struggle in which Socrates took part at Athens was the renewal at much closer quarters of the previous struggle in the foreign wars; in it, we said, the Greek found himself face to face with himself, as his own strongest enemy; and if that view of the case was the right one, then the victory of Socrates, of the Greek over himself, ought somehow to revert to the earlier conflict and prove to be also, not a repulse, but a complete conquest of the very barbarians, disguised in whom the Greek had first attacked himself and been so brilliantly routed. The later victory must have included and perfected the former. But exactly such a reversion did take place. Socrates' death, we shall find, proved to be in fact, as well as in the ideal or the spirit of it, a conquest or a sure promise of the conquest of the barbarians.

How best to make this clear I hardly know, and yet the task ought not to be so very difficult. It is not quite enough to say that Socrates widened Greece into Rome and that Rome included in her empire the barbarian enemies of Greece; nor does it suffice to point out that the Greek colonists, having so much of the spirit or motive that we have identified with Socrates, did but at first retreat before the danger of destruction as if in order later, as Romans, to return from the west and conquer rather than merely drive away the enemy. These are indications, but any complete explanation must go deeper.

Colonization and political centralization, as Greece herself has shown, and as history in many other instances has made manifest, are the two natural ways of defence and preservation at a moment of national danger. The centripetal movement and the centrifugal movement, moreover, we have seen, are not so much two movements as two phases of one. But these ways are obviously only means to repulse; they are not means to complete conquest; and why is this? Simply because in either there is a certain inconsistency, a contradiction, that shows the defence offered to be an imperfect one, and that therefore must modify or limit the success. Thus, as to the inconsistency, the colonist seems to say: "I am quite independent of place and tradition; I can go to the west, taking my household goods and my gods with me, and there continue to be myself;" but is it not perfectly clear that, if he were truly so independent, he would not need to move, he would not need to leave his birthplace at all? He contradicts himself when he goes down to his ship. Similarly, as to the contradiction in the other way of defence, political centralization must be in terms of something more than a geographical centre, if it is to bring about a real unity. A geographical capital implies also an assertion of independence of place, but it realizes itself through use of a particular place. Clearly in the face of such contradiction, defence can end only in repulse. Conquest, the limit, the perfection of repulse, can come only if the independence that colonization and political centralization assume is real and absolute. In the history of life about the Mediterranean, however, such absolute independence of space and time, of locality and tradition, was asserted in just the two events which we are endeavoring to connect,—the death of Socrates and the far-reaching empire of Rome. Socrates taught, and in his death enacted what he taught, that there was a higher selfhood than the selfhood of the place and the moment; and Rome, not less magnificent in her assertion, was established on the idea of a universal empire to be maintained not so much through the city of Rome, as a geographical capital, as through the Roman law, in which of course distinctions of place and time were transcended. Socrates and Rome, under whom repulse passed into conquest, represent the two original ways of defence, the centralization and the colonization, perfected; they show the very principle of defence set free and become fully effective. Socrates said and enacted, as if in the spirit of those who had identified motion with rest, " Perfect colonization is staying just where you are; " and Rome put a check upon colonization and gave a new interpretation to centralization by proclaiming: " Wherever man is, he is a Roman." In the legal status that every man in the empire, or for that matter, too, every man out of it, was given by Rome, freedom of space and time was asserted. Rome did but make her subjects positions or " measures " absolutely.

So we see what Socrates achieved, or at least the promise there was in his achievement. His victory did revert to the early struggles of his country; in him the earlier enemies were completely overcome. In his individual career, then, Socrates enacted what Rome in her larger repetition of Socrates' life subsequently accomplished; and whether we see the later process as the death of Greece or as the rise of Rome, the repetition of Socrates' self-expression is beyond question, and, whatever grandeur is to be seen in the power and extent of Rome, in that he had a share.

III.

But Rome was not built in a day, and our first interest at this time is rather in the death of Greece as a repetition of the death of Socrates than in the rise of Rome. So, having seen the larger implication of Socrates' achievement, we have again to return to Athens, the unhappy city destined to outgrow herself.

Our last view of Athens was, if you remember from the former chapter, of a city of misers, among whom had arisen as their most natural contemporary a reformer, and who with perfect naturalness eventually put their would-be reformer to death. By misers we meant hoarders instead of spenders or users of the sensuous life, while in the reformer we saw one who as unduly exalted the end of selfhood as his miserly fellows were exalting the means. All this we dwelt upon at some length. But with our present interest in Greek activity after the execution we have now to ask ourselves just what occurred at Athens in the days following the departure of Socrates. Socrates had made himself felt; nay, he had made himself active in the life of his people; he had stimulated into expression by them a dormant motive. But with what result or in what way did the change show itself among them?

Certainly after that expression, in which not only Socrates but also in him his assailants were condemned, Athens could not remain what she had been; with the motive which Socrates had set free become active in her life, a change had to show itself. Socrates did what Arnold von Winkelried did; and not less successfully, except that in the case of the Swiss patriot the action was much more rapid: he made his assailants die with him, using them, as was said above, for his own complete self-expression; but just how?

In this way, and perhaps the very reverse of what many would expect, forgetting how human mankind must always be; in a way that will seem to take the Greeks farther than ever from Socrates instead of nearer to him. Thus the effect of Socrates upon Athens was to make the people turn the miserly, sensuous life that they had been leading rather unreflectively than consciously, into an avowed ideal. He simply made them resolve to be what they had been.

Nothing could have been more natural. Nothing could have been more fatal. In so insisting upon continuing to be themselves, in setting before themselves their former life as henceforth a consciously held ideal, a unifying principle, they gave up the case *in toto* to their condemned reformer, since unity was just that for which Socrates had died. They showed themselves, then, hypnotized into dying with him. They testified to his after-life in them. Thus, in detail, they had been selfish, sensuous, seekers of individual momentary pleasure and advantage, but now they made pleasure their goal or standard, and, if you will reflect a little, you cannot but see that seeking pleasure consciously is a very different thing indeed from getting it or having it. No one, so thoroughly as a self-conscious pleasure-seeker, is taken out of the positive, practical, concrete relations of life; ever less reality adheres to things in which before the self-consciousness he had taken so much delight; he finds himself aloof as a result of his resolution to continue in active relation. The Greek pleasure-seekers came to deny Athens and Athenian life as completely as their inimitable teacher had done. Indeed, some of them, more alive to the fatal paradox into which Socrates had drawn them, said directly that pain, not pleasure, separation from the world and its ties, not identification with it, was the right standard of life; and one, namely, Plato, the most faithful pupil of the master, withdrew from positive relations to life generally into a select school of philosophy, the Academy, and there taught the withdrawal that he had so enacted. Abstraction, meditation, reminiscence, he said, was the way to live; and, expressing the same thing in his remarkable dialogues in which the life of Socrates was dramatically reproduced, he taught through them about a world of the One, of the immaterial but substantial Idea, in which justice was really justice, and selfhood was free from the bondage of particular places and particular moments. The conscious pleasure-seekers, you see, and the Academy of Plato, in spite of their reputed opposition, were perfectly natural contemporaries, being advocates of one and the same principle; they were as naturally contemporaries as their forerunners, the misers and the reformer, had been. In its two complementary aspects they disclose to us the continuance of the Greek's struggle with himself, and give signs of its end; they show that larger repetition of the Socratic activity in which we are here interested setting in strongly, irresistibly.

Now, if you will look closely at this later Athens of Plato[1] and the pleasure-seekers, you cannot fail to see there an invitation or a positive preparation for a well-known event in Greek history, — the rise of the Macedonian power under Philip

---

[1] Plato had reason enough to teach metempsychosis. Was not the Greek leaving his own body, his own institutions, his own peculiar life in all its phases? Was not his body, or his civilization, already beginning to crumble? Whither could Plato have him go, if not into another body or another civilization? The fact is, too, that into another civilization he did go.

and his son Alexander the Great. When a people abstracts itself, when it withdraws from the positive relations of its life, when it divorces means and end even to the point of stopping both its hoarding on the one side, — the hitherto active misers becoming reflective pleasure-seekers, — and its spending on the other, — the early activity of reform turning aside from the streets and market-places and entering a school, — then must ensue, not cessation of activity altogether, but larger activity or activity in which the very divorce of means and end among the people will be fulfilled, that is to say, the end of which will enter from without and make use of the unused means. In fact, a veritable evolution ensues. And just such a fulfilment or evolution of Plato's time, Philip and Alexander effected; they took Athens at her word, applying or enacting what she thought; they demonstrated that divorce of means and end at Athens meant their union in a process, an historical movement, quite inclusive of Athens, in a word, that Plato's Athens had quite outgrown herself.

And upon the union of means and end, Aristotle, the third great Socratic philosopher, insisted; but Aristotle, tutor to Alexander and protégé of the Macedonian court, did not develop his thought from the standpoint of one, like Plato, living in Athens, but from that of those political changes that were drawing Athens into a life as much deeper as it was more extensive than her life had been. Aristotle, in every branch of his philosophy, which he made so extensive and so varied that it seemed as if he intended to rival Alexander in its domain, taught that selfhood is realized by no withdrawal from material conditions, but rather by adjustment to them or action in them; selfhood is their perfection or fulfilment; the soul is not an end by itself, but the end or purpose of the body. Thus, as showing at once the wider and the more practical and worldly standpoint of Aristotle's ideas, there is his notion of the state as having its basis, not in some philosopher's dream, not in some far-off Utopia, where Plato imagined it, not in an unworldly somewhere, but in so real and present and practical a thing as the human family. In the human family the state was a means unto itself as end. Of course distinctly Athenian institutions had to fall before that idea; but after all the idea was of their own developing, and certainly nothing could have been more perfectly in line with the efforts of Alexander to spread his empire to the east and the south and wherever the human family could be found.

The practical way, furthermore, in which Aristotle interpreted Plato to himself, or in which

Macedonia fulfilled Athens, revealing her evolution to her, has still another side. Thus to Macedonia as the direct agent in the process now before us, and Aristotle as the accompanying interpreter or philosopher of it, we owe the clear notion of the world as the embodiment or the incarnation of reason, or, more technically, the doctrine of the λόγος, or Word Incarnate. Athens, outgrowing herself, separated end and means, mind and matter, soul and body; but Macedonia, as has been shown, enacting and fulfilling that outgrowth, brought these factors together again. Athens developed an abstract learning; but Macedonia carried Greek learning wherever she went with her conquering armies, turning the once despised barbarians not merely into Greek subjects, but often into Greek sages. Under Alexander she founded the city of Alexandreia in Egypt, and there Greek wisdom came into relation with Hebrew wisdom, and each thought it had discovered itself anew. Reason so long shut up in Athens found herself the right and privilege of man the world over, a property of the world rather than a conceit of the Greek; and in his doctrine of the λόγος, the world-reason, Aristotle gave a philosopher's recognition of this change.

But Socrates would not have been content with the empire of Alexander; and Greece, in whom the Socratic motive was now active, was not. The Greek's victory over himself had to be still more complete. Had he not shown this himself when he assisted Hannibal against Rome? His individual selfhood, broadened as it had been by the recent events, was still his, whereas a universal selfhood was his inevitable because his self-determined goal. In his very learning, that Macedonia fostered so faithfully, he still kept himself in so far aloof; he still confused means and end; he was not perfectly free as means to himself, as end. Yet how could such freedom come? Surely only through his taking literally the doctrine of the world-reason, and therein resigning his individual reason completely; only through his entrance into an empire other than the Macedonian, in no wise Greek, for which Greek ideas and Greek institutions would have no intrinsic value. When, then, in the middle of the second century before Christ, Greece became a Roman province, the accomplishment of this more perfect freedom was all but at hand, the only drawback being that not until some years later was Rome herself altogether free. And in this conquest, I must reiterate, Rome did but take Greece at her word, even as Macedonia had taken Athens. In each case it was as if the conqueror had said to the conquered, "Not to destroy, but to fulfil." "To die is gain,"

Socrates had said in his last words before his judges, when the verdict of death had been passed upon him.

But Greece resisted Rome, some one says in objection to this easy-going way of taking most tragic events of history, and also efforts had been made earlier to throw off the Macedonian yoke. Very true; but so did even the man Socrates rise up to defend himself against his assailants. No great change is without a struggle, but we seek here a view of history that is deeper than battles and leagues and mere conquests. Our own life is not without its struggles, and that of Greece was not; but still, to repeat a now familiar assertion, the death of Greece, like the death of her prophet Socrates, was far from self-denial, it was more perfect self-expression. Had not the ideal of Rome first showed itself in Alexander? And did not Alexander bring into material expression and so realize an ideal born in Athens?

IV.

It was said a moment ago that the Greek to fulfil himself must take Aristotle's doctrine of the world-reason literally, sacrificing his own individual reason wholly. This seems to mean that he must abandon his science and philosophy and conceit of knowledge in any form; and what else could it mean but that? Had not Socrates himself exalted the conviction of ignorance far above any assumption of knowledge? To be sure, after Socrates had come Plato, with his monumental system of philosophy; but Plato and the general attitude of abstraction in his times were only natural predecessors of Macedonia and Aristotle. Yes, the Greek had no final choice but avowal of ignorance. The reason was, after all, the world's, not his. The ultimate effect of Socrates and Plato was to make him purely passive and intellectually receptive. Abstraction in thought and life, conviction that truth is a report, not of this, but of some other world, with which we have no direct connection, upon which we have no hold through our senses, must ever end so. After reminiscence comes revelation.

The Greek went to the east and to the south, and found his own thought in others; and while the first feeling that came to him was one of triumph, the second was one of submission. Rome followed Macedonia in his mental as well as in his political life. In Athens, although the Academy lived long after Plato, its philosophy rapidly developed from the beautiful system that Plato had conceived to a more serious, because a so much deeper, scepticism than Socrates had ever to contend with, and at Alexandreia, where the Greek was so much freer from himself, as a result of the thought interchange, particularly between the Hebrews and the Greeks, there arose a philosophy, that had its advocates abroad as well, to the east in Syria and to the west in Rome, in which such mystical ways of arriving at truth as "swooning into the absolute" came to be taught. Truth was regarded as something that must come; it was no longer something to be sought. It belonged to the world, remember; not to man.

In the life of such as still retained some practical hold on reality, whether at Rome or at Athens, two distinctly moral systems of thought, in which essentially the same mental attitude was present, found support, namely, Stoicism and Epicureanism; both expressing one interest and need of life, but from opposite sides. Thus the Stoic dwelt upon the idea that the reason was wholly the world's, perfect conformity or submission to it being the only way to happiness. "The condition of mind to be sought after," he declared, "is apathy;" "pain is no evil;" "nothing can happen contrary to the will of the wise man." But Epicurus and his following dwelt, not on reason as the world's, but on reason as not man's. Man, they said, has in himself no rational part, no nature to survive his sensuous consciousness;

pleasure here on earth is his natural goal; with no responsibility to any other than the sensuous life, what has he to fear but himself? Any other fear — above all, the fear of death — is idle; and, to quote at some length from Epicurus himself:

"The knowledge that death has nothing to do with us makes what is mortal in life truly enjoyable, not because it adds to life immortality, but because it takes away our longing for immortality. For there is nothing which can terrify a man in life when he is assured that nothing is terrible in the absence of life. So that he is a fool who tells us to fear death, not because its presence will torment us, but that its anticipation torments us. For that which troubles us not when it is come has vain terrors for us when it is looked forward to. Death, then, the most awful of ills, is nothing in our eyes; for, when we are, death is not, and when death is, we are not."[1]

With such bold resignation the Epicureans were even better Stoics than the Stoics themselves; the reason, or law, or undying nature, that was not man's but the world's, the Epicureans wished to forget altogether. Indeed, as if catching this implication, alike of Stoicism and of Epicureanism, some especially original thinkers of the day set

[1] Translation from W. L. Courtney's Studies in Philosophy, p. 48.

up an absolute forgetfulness as the only road to reality.

But such attitudes of mind show Aristotle's devotion to the world-reason in application. All in their several ways expressive of submission, they show how in the history of Greece, as well as in that of Mediterranean life generally, man was becoming literally a means to an end, and, too, a means to himself, his deeper, truer self, as the real end, since, as we have seen particularly in the case of the Greeks, the change had more than an external cause. A motive lying deep in the Greek character had required it; a motive, present in Greek life and thought from the beginning, strengthening with time and experience, and finally revealed and brought into social expression by the life and death of Socrates, had demanded this evolution of man as means, his ready submission to an end quite apart from himself, in that his own sensuous consciousness had no claim upon it, his perfect conviction of ignorance and helplessness, and politically his acceptance of a legally determined position in the empire of military Rome. Taking Aristotle's world-reason literally, — he had to take it so for his own self-being, — he became but one in an organized army, in whose movements we see the very principle for which Socrates had died at last set free, — the principle, namely, of a universal self, or a common humanity, or of an end in life that transcends the life of the body, making the body naught but part of a great mechanism.

But we see more than this. It will be remembered that upon observing carefully the Athens of Socrates' time we had to believe in Socrates almost before we really found him in person among the people. Now, however, in the events and thoughts of these later times another necessity of belief is forced upon us. The fall of Greece, which has been to us but a repetition or a fulfilment of the death of Socrates, the scepticism, the resignation, the individual lost in a mechanism the end of whose activity must have seemed to each single creature living in it not of this world at all, — else the movement could never be as free as the times and changes required, — the fall of Greece, the second death of Socrates in the conquest of his race, with all its incidents, was the birth of Christ. St. Augustine, with unconscious subtlety, writing some years later, epitomized the whole story, the scepticism and all, the death and the birth, when he gave his proof of the existence of God. In brief: *Fallor, ergo Deus est;* man's deception, man's blindness, is revelation of God's existence. History, you see, lived or enacted that proof, long before the great Church father discovered any validity in it. *Fallor* — that is the death of Socrates, — " I know that I do not know; " *ergo Deus est* — that is the birth of Christ — in Rome, — " He that loseth his life for my sake shall find it." Not self-denial, however, let us keep in mind, but self-expression was in the death of Socrates.

V.

You do not see the necessity of Christ, whether in St. Augustine's logic or in the history that it unwittingly epitomized so wonderfully? Then, again, reflect a little. The history shows: Reason no longer man's, but the world's; forgetfulness, the successor of reason in man; man himself become but a means to the world's end; universal empire; militarism or mechanism; and, finally, action or movement, since the mechanism was hardly at rest. But this action or movement — what of it? It did what action always does: it made the conditions that determined its possibility or that set it free, — it made those conditions ideal; and ideal in no visionary way, since the action had proved the ideal alive.

And what, to repeat, was the ideal, the living reality of which the action or movement of military Rome revealed? What was its content or its gospel? Why, as already suggested, exactly what the history showed: the self as means, forgetfulness, reason as not man's but the world's, and the rest, except that of necessity the action or the movement turned these into self-denial instead of merely self as means, faith in or revelation of the world's reason instead of forgetfulness, and freedom instead of slavery to mechanism. The action did but glorify its conditions.

But in these later terms the revealed ideal, living, active, upon the earth, was Christ, liberator of the world, the world-reason, the Word Incarnate, the supreme example of self-denial. In the very movement of Rome's armies, then, in the action of the legally established mechanism, lay the necessity of Christ, or the real cogency of St. Augustine's proof. Romans had no choice but to believe in Christ. Did they not believe in themselves? To the Greeks Paul could preach an unknown God, worshipped by them but in ignorance; but to the Romans, only a God the principle of whose nature was already the basis of the authority of their Imperator, the sanction and motive of their Roman life, the law that they were unto themselves.

Plainly the Christ to which we refer was more than the individual character of history; he was more than the Jewish reformer. Just as we have spoken of Socrates in a deeper sense than that having reference to the martyred Greek at Athens, so has Christendom always thought of Christ in a deeper sense than that with reference to Christ the Jew.

In the history of the Jews themselves the idea of Christ passed through several stages. He was, as we know, first a world-ruling Messiah, a King who was to come and give the Jews, so long inured to captivity, a mastery over all nations; secondly, he was, in a more spiritual sense, a Saviour, but a Saviour only of the Jews; thirdly, he was Saviour of the World, as if in response to the Roman conquest of his people; and, finally, — and this at the crowning moment of his death, that that death might also mean self-expression, not self-denial, — he was the vital principle of salvation; reason on Earth; God, not a man among men, but a motive at last real and active in humanity; not an abstract principle, as some, too ready to refuse to Christ any objective reality, any reality save that of an inspiring idea, have tried to imagine, but a freed and a freeing activity, that was as real and as far-reaching as the life of Rome. And of course there was a remarkable fitness in the revelation of this saving activity coming to the Roman world through a Jew. The Jewish people throughout their history were a people of captivities. Over and over again they had lived through just the experience which Roman arms at last brought to the Mediterranean life. They had been evolved so; that is, by ever being involved. What more natural than that the great teacher for all the captive peoples of the conquering empire should appear at Jerusalem? Not only did the conditions of history require his birth, but also they required his birth there; and, lest I be seriously misunderstood, when I say that history *required* it there, let me add that no such thing as determinism is for a moment intended, but this, namely, that in that history, as in all history, we find what man was, and so what his very selfhood, his own self-being, required. That were strange history, indeed, which told us what man had to be wholly in spite of himself, as if human action in response to conditions were possible without the equally real existing human motive.

It will complete the story of these chapters if we bring to mind the twofold way in which Rome herself came to receive the Christian revelation. To Rome, — and what else could we expect, knowing the central part that political Rome played in this development? — to Rome, as already hinted, the gospel of incarnation meant something temporal as well as something spiritual: it meant a Pope, with claims to temporal power, as well as a Christ; or a Pope in whom Emperor and Christ should be one. If Christianity through captive Judea said to Greece and to the other conquered peoples that even in the captivity was supreme opportunity, that such self-denial was through an already accomplished self-expression, to successful Rome she said — for on no other terms could Rome have accepted her teaching — that in the Emperor dwelt also the Christ, God's representative on earth.

But we have, or probably seem to have, wandered far from our subject, "The Death of Socrates." Yet from what the death of Socrates came finally to mean to us we have not wandered at all, — unless any conclusion may be said to be a departure from its premises. We have only left our premises in order, as we close, to dwell, rather too briefly than at too great length or with too much digression, upon this conclusion. The death of Socrates, then, with its fulfilment in the fall of Greece, was the birth of Christ with its fulfilment in the freedom of Rome, at once a temporal and a spiritual power. So did history forestall St. Augustine in proving God. And, finally, Socrates' "I know that I do not know," with all the incidents of thought and life that we have seen to belong to it, turned, by the force of its own logic, through the liberation of its own deeper motive, into *Deus est*, God is alive on earth.

Part II.

THE DEATH OF CHRIST.

CHAPTER I.

JUDEA.

I.

WE have now seen the closest connection between the death of Socrates and the birth of Christ. We have found that the lives of the two men were vital incidents in the unfolding of human experience. In the wonderful logic of history they appeared to us inseparable. Thus the death of Socrates was the birth of Christ. In their different ways, too, — Socrates in the way already disclosed to us, and Christ in a way hardly unseen before but now to be made clear, — they were witnesses to will and motive and individual responsibility in history. If Socrates, himself a Greek, forestalled Rome in the conquest of Greece, Christ, as much Roman as Jew, by his life and death overcame Rome, and won for himself the right to be called the prophet of modern life.

In the study of Socrates we had only the ordinary difficulties of all study, but here in the study before us, although we have been led to it so naturally, a difficulty confronts us that we felt only distantly, if at all, before. To most, if not to all, Socrates has never been more than a figure in ancient history, interesting perhaps to the scholar, but hardly vitally important to the man. Christ, however, lives to-day, and is close to the hearts of millions of people, and his being so real and so near makes the study of him, the quiet scrutiny of his life and death, not only hard but also in the thought of many unnecessary and undesirable. So many whose feelings one wants to respect, think that what one is justified in saying of him has been wholly determined beforehand. They even expect the use of certain conventional phrases, — a Christian emotion rather than a Christian understanding being the only aim that they can give countenance to.

But no one will deny that it is always the truth that sets men free. Indeed, I find myself only repeating here what was said before. Cherished ideals have nothing to fear from the study of life's deepest concerns. Rather they have everything to gain. Accordingly, whatever is real and abiding in the relation of Christ to man will only be brought nearer to completion and realization by a clear knowledge of it, reached through independent study. In fact, one has to think but little to lose one's sympathy with those who are so short-sighted as to determine beforehand what they will admit to their thinking and as to discourage or possibly to resent the more candid thinking of others; and for my own part also the very position of such over-cautious people makes an undertaking like the present seem only just so much the more worth while. Still I would make my study, however independent, however critical, so simple and so direct that my present defence of it will be justified, and the work itself, seem at its close, not an attack at all, but an interpretation.

We have found that Christ was more than an idea. He was a motive, a principle of salvation, which the rise of Roman supremacy set free in humanity. That motive, however, we saw, not from the standpoint of the life that gave its name, but from that of a life rather pagan than Christian; and while the motive itself must be deeper than any distinction between paganism and Christianity, yet the fullest appreciation requires a view of it in its Jewish as well as in its Greek setting. Indeed, only as we get an idea of the life and character of the Jews can we understand how in Christ the motive was so much more fully expressed and human nature so much more clearly defined, and how Christ's conquest was so much wider than Socrates', being as much of the Romans as of his own people. We must fully understand Christ the Jew before we can understand Christ the motive or saving principle. We must understand the life at Jerusalem before we can understand the life in the hearts of men from the days of Christ's coming to the present time.

Christ's conquest was double; as just now said, it was of Romans as well as of Jews. Of its double character we had a hint before. Thus you remember how the selfhood of Christ passed in men's thoughts from the Jewish Messiah to the life and heart of Rome. St. Paul, in his Epistle to the Romans, saw Christ as the law which a man is unto himself, or as one in whom all, being many, are yet "one body," being "every one members one of another;" and, as we saw, the selfhood of Christ came even to be identified with the Roman Emperor. But, after such identification, how was it possible that Rome should not repeat in her imperial career the sacrifice at Jerusalem, even as Greece had repeated the sacrifice at Athens? The death of Socrates and the fall of Greece were one; and so, too, the death of Christ and the fall of Rome; and if in the former was the birth of imperialism, in the latter, as we shall find when we have followed it out to its fullest meaning, was the birth of whatever is deepest and most real in life to-day.

So in the pages that are still before us our interest is, first, in the death of Christ at Jerusalem; secondly, in Rome's repetition of it; and, finally, in whatever Rome's downfall realized for both the national and the individual life of our own times.

II.

In the history of civilization it was the peculiar part of Christ's people, the Jews, to take captivity captive. Their history, a long record of captivities, prepared them for such a part, and mankind naturally looked to them for help when captivity and empire became general over the earth. But what we have to notice is that the Jews took captivity captive, not only in the way of Christ, as everywhere recognized, but also in another way, a peculiarly worldly way, that has not been generally recognized. We have been too ready to forget that Christ himself was a Jew, and that therefore, however great, however spiritual his achievement, the Jewish people, even in their opposition to him, must have shared in it.

Yes, the Jews did, albeit in a way quite their own, what Christ did; they, as well as he, overcame Rome, and at the very height of her imperial glory. What their own way was we shall see, in course of time, and we shall find, too, that it has been as much a part of the progress of civilization as Christ's way; but, for the present, I wish to dwell on the bare fact, which I now express in these words, that, in so far as Christ was a Jew, the Jews themselves must have been Christians, — Christians, perhaps, in spite of themselves, but still Christians. At the Crucifixion, indeed, when on the little hill west of Jerusalem, alike in the self-sacrificing prophet and in the sacrificing people, the Jewish nature found its culminating expression, the exchange of characters was complete. At the Crucifixion the Jew died; the Christian survived.

Does this sound strange? To some, no doubt, it is even harsh. But the relation of a great leader to his people can hardly be anything else than this of exchange of characters. Socrates exemplified it; and the fact is that I should hardly have resorted to so great a paradox, if our Greek studies had not already prepared us for it. Those studies gave us, as a tool for use in the interpretation of history, the principle of the identity, or at least of the symmetry, of opposites. Thus, in what sense the misers and the spendthrift-reformer at Athens, or after them the would-be pleasure-seekers and Plato with his Utopian ideas, or finally the Greeks as Macedonian subjects and Aristotle with his world-reason, were contemporaries by nature, being in sympathy even in spite of themselves, we know through this principle. They were natural contemporaries, in that in spite of their opposition or rather because of it they contained, each opposite side in itself, the same contradiction, being symmetrical expressions of that contradiction, being each rather in conflict with itself than with its opponent, and expressing in one or another of the different stages the Greek's long conflict with himself. The opposing sides seemed so truly to co-operate in freeing the national motive that we might almost have spoken of the Greek race as seizing upon its trouble and working out its salvation with its two hands. But, the action and achievement of the Greeks aside, the same co-operation of symmetrical opposites was in the character and activity of Christ the crucified and of the Jews his crucifiers.

And what is opposition but a process in which opponents mediate each other's activities? Did contestants ever fail in their struggle to change sides? Shakespeare, in his " Merchant of Venice," has given a suggestion of what opposition and conflict involve. He, indeed, sets Christian against Jew; but, before the play is ended, remembering the standards of the time, one has in Portia the better Jew, and in submissive Shylock the more perfect Christian. Simply, Shylock is out-Jewed; Portia is out-Christianed. So I say, again, that at the Crucifixion, in a very real sense, the Jews and Christ changed sides, or came each to express the nature of the other. The Jews in their way and Christ in his way took captivity captive.

Quantum sufficit. You bid me now explain. Just in what way did the Jewish people overcome Rome?

III.

WELL, the Jew is probably more widely known than any other national type. Very significantly he has spread over the world, either in person or in character and social function, as rapidly and as widely as Christianity. He has been generally despised; but certainly, whatever the feeling about him, birth made him what he was, and Christianity has contributed largely towards making him what he is, and at most he can be but an intensification of something real in the character of us all. Indeed, to revert to the paradox, when one thinks a little, how is it possible, with Christ himself a Jew, that all who call themselves Christians should not in some way be Jews also?

Traditionalism and a disposition to a somewhat peculiar form of idolatry are the Jew's original marks, and in view of his long life of wandering and dependence neither is to be wondered at. The nomadic life, the years in the desert, the submission to Egypt and Syria and Babylon, to Persia and Macedonia, and finally to Rome, made him treasure his past, its traditions and such outer emblems of it as he could carry with him, as no other has ever done; and he came, ever more and more, because so much in his life was determined for him, because he was so much more involved than evolved, to think of the authority of his own ideals and emblems as quite external to him. In short, his past became an idol, and what could have been more natural? It became an idol, too, not one whit less exacting than the alien kings and princes that ruled over him, so that in worshipping it he did but make a captive of his captive self, identifying his opportunity of self-expression with his necessity.

Now, between the Jewish worshipper of the past and the Greek miser or hoarder of it there was a most important difference. The Jew clung to relics; the Greek erected monuments. The Jew regarded the records and emblems of his life as possessing an intrinsic worth; the Greek found worth only where his senses were stimulated.

For the Jew the past was a sacred inheritance to be kept; for the Greek it was a feeling to be revived. The difference between the symbolic and the artistic or between the formal and the pleasing, or, if regard is had to their effects on national character, between a country of plains and deserts and a country of mountain barriers and islands, was the difference between Jew and Greek.

Furthermore, although political supremacy was denied the Jew, his national spirit, refusing to be crushed, found satisfaction in a theocracy. Indeed, to be subject to alien rulers, to be idolatrous of the past, and to be chosen of God were inseparable conditions of the Jew's life. In priests and prophets he found a substitute for what in the way of political control the monarchs of the East never allowed him. In faith and insight and revelation, in signs and miracles, he found a substitute for the reason that so signally characterized the Greek. And can it be that the sole difference between faith and reason, or between theocracy and autonomy, is a matter merely of length of time, or of frequency in a given time, in which an experience comes? Surely our thinking here has suggested some such conclusion. The following formula, as almost mathematically true, has been urging itself upon us for expression and reflection: In as many centuries as the Greeks were occupied in their conquest of themselves, for so many times did the children of Israel live through the same tragic experience. For the Jews, especially in their political life, a thousand years were as one day, and one day as a thousand years.

So, very briefly, we find the Jews, — unlike the Greeks, but unlike because the same life and character so often repeated, so much intensified; idolaters, not misers; believers, not thinkers; guardians of an idea, not long struggling and far-seeking discoverers of it; God's chosen people; and in history, in their special way, conquerors, not mere subjects of Rome.

IV.

IN Christ's time the Jews had brought their idolatry of the past to the point of a perfect paradox, that is to say, to the moment of precipitation. Throughout their history they had not only worshipped the past, but also dreamt of a Messiah; and obviously the worship and the dream were inseparable attitudes of mind. But at the time of Christ's coming the past had ceased to be the object of reverence that it had been, and in consequence the dream of the future had also lost its hold. The temple had become a place for money-changers, and worship was rather a form than a spiritual emotion. The paradox, then, was this. The traditionalism and the idolatry, of course of their own weight or from their own nature, had changed to sheer formalism, which is always so much more than it seems. To use the metaphor again, formalism brings precipitation. Formalism is the past coming into actual use. It is at once acting in the future and looking at the past, or a sort of advancing backward. It is a seizing opportunity and pretending pious duty or necessity. It is practice wholly out of accord with teaching. And when such a contradiction is reached in a people's development or conflict with itself, a birth is at hand.

The past become formal, what else can it mean but the future become real and living, free and active, in the present; and the future, free and living, what but birth and individuation? Such necessity of birth and individuation we have seen at Athens; now we see it again at Jerusalem. As at Athens, moreover, so at Jerusalem; as the reformer to the misers, so the Messiah to the idolaters; the Messiah, like the reformer, was himself under the spell of the contradiction that gave him birth. Thus, just such a separation or abstraction as his people made of the past he made of the future. He and they were opposites, but symmetrical opposites. He was under the spell of the contradiction that bound them, and to the contradiction his death, viewed as his own act or as his people's, was due.

Thus, in order that what we have here may arrange and define itself in our thought, I say, with little more than repetition, that the Jewish idolaters had come to insist upon retaining for life at Jerusalem a content that was no longer real or no longer vitally stimulating,— hence their formalism; and that the Messiah undertook to express in life an as yet unrealized ideal; hence his character as Messenger from another World; and, finally, that, just because their traditionalism and his idealism were both under the spell of essentially the same contradiction, or were aspects of one activity of a people's life, or were each only a counter-manifestation and so a deeper manifestation of the other, and because the continued expression of the activity had ever to deepen or intensify each of its aspects, — for just these reasons were the crucifixion and the self-sacrifice, as the two sides of the culminating expression of the Jewish character, necessary in history. Only so could the ideal be realized; only so could the national motive be set finally free. From one side, that of the people, the past, from the other, that of Christ, the future, was brought into adjustment with the present. As in all adjustment, as at the moment of realization of any ideal, the future died that the past might fulfil itself in the present.

It would hardly do, as you must see, to recount the Jew's struggle with himself as resulting from a confusion of means and end. The terms means and end, as commonly used, were well fitted to the Greeks; but the Jews were not artisans nor fighters nor great leaders, their activity being of a less worldly sort. More direct than means and end are the terms suggested, past and future, or, to give still others, letter and spirit. These show the conflict of just such a people as we have seen the Jews to be, of a people that had lived and moved and had its being within an activity quite inclusive of its own. Means and end, moreover, are the concern of reason; letter and spirit, or past and future, of faith; and the Jews were a people of faith. Thus, if in still another way the Jews may be distinguished from the Greeks, we find at Jerusalem, instead of a time-serving knowledge, instead of individual man as the measure of all things, a belief no deeper than words and ceremonies, and instead of an intellectual awakening through a knowledge of ignorance, a spiritual revival through a conviction of personal insufficiency, that is to say, instead of "I know that I do not know," "I believe, help thou mine unbelief." Not against subjectivism and utilitarianism and pleasure-seeking did Christ set himself, but against such vain conceits as an empty faith and a hollow spiritual life.

V.

Now at the Crucifixion the Jew's formalism, with its empty faith and hollow spiritual life, came into use; it came into use completely, explicitly. So to speak, with the special view of life, the character and the history that it implied, it became a finished and actually useful tool; it became an *instrumental* formalism, that is, something more than a mere state of mind, say an attitude of defined self-expression or a basis of positive action. In fact, the Crucifixion did nothing more nor less than give the Jew a trade or profession, of whose activity it was itself typical. For consider —

I have described the Jew's formalism as at once acting in the future and looking at the past or as a sort of walking backwards, and I have shown how the birth of Christ was involved in it. But at his death Christ made fully manifest the nature of formalism; he revealed the future as its ideal or motive; and he made his people, even in their opposition to him, adopt his Christian standpoint. He made them face about. He gave them a future. He defined their formalism by giving it an end, sacrificing himself to it that they might be set free.

They had been idolaters of the past and had become formalists, but at the Crucifixion they were brought to the point of affirming that the future was their motive with exactly the same emphasis that Christ himself used. In treating him as an impostor they had no choice but to become loyal at least to the principle for which he stood. If he was not their Messiah, then the Messiah was still to come; and upon their return to this forgotten and all but lifeless faith the formalism that had been developed among them became instrumental, and they came into a trade or profession. They were transformed, as if by magic, from idolaters and traditionalists into lenders. The Crucifixion itself was an act of lending.

Of course a state of mind, as it becomes defined, must always imply the development of some material interest, the setting in of some specially chosen social function. In other words, when it becomes a basis of positive action, when it becomes instrumental, it assumes of necessity some material expression. The Jewish formalism, changing in the way that we have seen, illustrates this. Being, as regards its verbal formulæ and its outer ceremonial, an altogether abstract basis of social intercourse, an wholly external medium of exchange, it created a mental attitude that was preparatory to admitting, as if at the back door, — a phrase confessedly more expressive than elegant, — a very worldly activity. Worldly activities often, if not always, enter in some such way; men choose to let them in so; and, in the case of the Jews, upon their growth into instrumental formalism their lending became money-lending. Obviously, money is but a material basis of formalism as medium of exchange or as liberated for the actual use of the world.[1]

Money, as a commodity abstracted and assigned an wholly intrinsic worth, is the past treasured solely for itself, and so embodied in a medium wholly external to its possessor; it is the past as so much coin or value for the present; it is that in which all developed wants and relations are become one and abstract, or that in which hunger and thirst and avarice of all kinds and desire of travel and longing for all sorts of opportunities have a common object; in a word, it is a material counterpart of the unity of the self or of a common or universal self in society. In money are we

---

[1] It is important to remember here that the Jews were naturally given to agriculture. They were not, naturally, before Christ's time, commercially disposed. Witness their laws against putting money on interest. See Lev. xxv. 36, 37, and Deut. xxiii. 20; also an article in the "International Journal of Ethics," "The Jewish Question," by Morris Jastrow, Jr., July, 1896.

all one. On earth in money, as hereafter in the Christian's Heaven, are we all one.[1]

And so, at last, in the Jews becoming by nature money-lenders we have the special way, the worldly way, in which they adopted Christianity, or in which they, like Christ himself, overcame Rome or took captivity captive. For, as just now indicated, money is a worldly counterpart of Heaven. Money-lending, too, demands a loyalty to what is regarded, even in our own times, as the distinctly Christian attitude of mind. Thus it relies, does it not? on an unseen future, on faith, on self-denial, on world-credit; and, strangely enough, so do the extremes meet, it is really an "unworldly" activity,

[1] And here, but in a note, I am tempted to a slight digression. There are two opposite theories in ethics, corresponding to the two sides of Christianity just indicated above, — to the money or Jew side and to the Heaven or Christ side. These two theories are hedonism and abstract or intuitional or indeterministic idealism. The former makes pleasure, the latter makes duty the natural motive of conduct. But pleasure *as motive or ideal* is a complete abstraction for the past as having value to the present, and duty is a complete abstraction for the future. Since, however, money is a perfect abstraction of the past, the thoroughly consistent hedonist should be a money-seeker, while the consistent idealist should be on his side a money-lender. Accordingly the two theories complement each other, and in banking are to be seen in co-operation, where money is lent for itself, and in the Christian Heaven, where duty is also pleasure. And, finally, St. Paul's message to the Athenians of a God worshipped in ignorance meant one thing to the pleasure-worshippers, making them the hirelings of Rome, and another to the opposing Platonists, making them believers in the Kingdom of Heaven.

a sort of unworldliness in the world itself, an abstracting of the world's business, or a worldly life that is quite apart from man's ordinary labors as productive and directly useful. In history, moreover, there have been two characters that have been conspicuous from the first for their ever-increasing independence of imperial Rome, — the Christian believer, namely, and the money-lender.

And I must add, in order to keep our ideas well together, that trading money for itself or lending it, money being what we have seen it to be, was the natural fulfilment of the motive which the long captivity of the Jews, the traditionalism and the theocracy, had nurtured. In money-lending the confusion of future with past found expression, and a national life, so long isolated, so long deprived of participation in distinctly worldly affairs, was set free, the people turning their necessity into opportunity. In money-lending theocracy was brought down to earth and shown to be expressive of an accomplished adjustment to secular life. I know well that to have been the chosen people of God and to have become dealers in money will seem to such as think only of the words or as get no farther than that "love of money is the root of all evil" an historical absurdity, and for the Jews wholly damnatory, but in reality it was, historically and psychologically, a necessity. Love of money may be "the root of all evil," but assuredly it is also a basis of most Christian possibilities; it is an indispensable condition of the evolution of a Christian society. The step from theocracy to banking was a very short one, as short as that from spirit to matter. The parable of the talents was peculiarly suited to the life and character of the Jews.[1]

Yes, at the Crucifixion, in their special way, a very worldly way, the Jews became Christians. In a way quite their own they were conquerors of Rome. The other world, with which they met the earthly claims of Rome, was indeed, in spite of the otherness, altogether worldly, but it dealt an effective blow. And theirs was, it is true, a Christianity only by a sort of analogy, say a physical or a "negative" Christianity or a Christianity rather in fact than in ideal, rather in in-

---

[1] And here a note. Somebody will doubtless remind me that I am in an important respect doing violence to history. Not so. My meaning is not that the Jews invented banking. Such an idea would be absurd. Nothing was ever *invented*. Babylon and Greece and early Rome had bankers, although treasure-keeping rather than banking appears to be the truer account of their business. The Jews invented banking no more than Christ invented Christianity. They only freed the principle to the world. Just as Socrates made the old-time militarism imperial and as Christ made the pre-Christian Christianity international, so the Jew made banking world-wide, and is, therefore, if any one would distinguish him, rather its presiding genius than its sole agent or creator.

stinct or force than in will; but its importance to human life and progressive civilization can hardly be overestimated.

VI.

ARE you now impatient with me for giving so much time to money and banking and so little time to Christ and the spiritual beauty and grandeur of his life and character? Do I seem trivial or even irreverent in the way in which I would interpret the great tragedy at Jerusalem? Yet, in answer, my feeling most certainly is not irreverent. As keenly as any one I appreciate all that was done for humanity at Christ's death; as fondly as any one I cherish all that was achieved by him for what we value most in life to-day. But, as you must see, I ever have to remember what in time past we have been disposed to forget and what accordingly we have failed properly to measure: I remember that Christ was a Jew; and, just because he was a Jew, I am constrained to think that the Jews as a nation shared in his achievement, as in general I have to think that for every spiritual advance in man's unfolding there must come also a material change, co-operating with it, not opposing it, as any instrument co-operates even with a complaining workman. As said already, money and banking, so natural to the Jewish character, have been, beyond all question, a material basis of Christian possibility. Even as Socrates, albeit against their will, drew his people unto himself, turning them from misers into pleasure-seekers and finally into selves as means in the use of pagan military Rome, so Christ, born of the life and longing of the Jews, drew the Jews unto himself, transforming the resentful idolaters into lenders of their abstracted and materialized past, and finally into bankers for the use of Christendom.

And it is certainly no objection to the position that I take here, that the Jews have been anti-Christian. It is, on the contrary, corroboration. Keep in mind that our present interest goes deeper than any mere opposition. If the Jews have been anti-Christian, in the last analysis it can be only because Christians themselves have been so too, thereby inviting the opposition. Even as Christ was a Jew, so have his followers been Jews also, and had the same struggle to pass through. Who hates the Jews should remember that it is always suicide to hate too strongly.

But my meaning will be finally clear, if I suggest in a paragraph or two in what ways Christians have shown themselves of a more or less Jewish character. And, to begin with, being Jewish is not in money-lending alone. What I have called instrumental formalism, essential to lending, is not confined to operations in money. Instrumental formalism is one and the same thing with a selfish sympathy, that is, a sympathy exercised only as a tool of individual self-interest; and wherever a selfish sympathy manifests itself, there is the Jew's lending with the abstraction of the future as motive. Or, conversely, living, not *for*, but *in* the future, as many seem to do, has the most natural effect of weakening responsibility to life and conditions as they are, and so of making possible, if not even of stimulating, a wholly selfish use of the present. Thus, Christians so often doing little more than dreaming of heaven have again and again trifled with their earthly responsibilities. They have stopped at sentimental charity, which is a crude selfishness. They have co-operated with institutions, notably political institutions, known to be corrupt. They have accepted for their work dishonestly won money. They have lost themselves in mere Sunday observance, in devotion to creeds and rituals. And in all these things that they have done who cannot see the selfish sympathy, the lender's interest, the Jew's instrumental formalism?

But, to show the same thing from still another side, I have heard it said by foreigners, that in this country the people are peculiarly dishonest, — that in politics, in education, in religion, we are most flagrant conventionalists; and although we are not the only people in Christendom upon whom this charge of conventionalism might be put, I think we can hardly complain of injustice when it is cast at us. Certainly it is dishonest for teachers and for preachers, as well as for politicians, to turn their backs on new truth, to temporize with new points of view, to know no future but the hereafter, in short, to be and to do a hundred and one things for the sake merely of present position and "influence" or from fear of stirring life too deeply. It is dishonest, and it shows the Jew cropping out. It is a cowardly abstraction of the future in order to avoid the incommodities of change in the present. It is mere banking, always bent on keeping things as they are, and so on giving to what is past an intrinsic value.

So are Christians in reality their own despised Jews, and the struggle of a Christian society is Christ's struggle. Christians have to struggle only with the Judaism in themselves. Witness the history of Christendom from its beginning to the present time.

VII.

But now, in summary, at the Crucifixion Christ in his way and his people in their way overcame Judaism. They overcame[1] Judaism, on the one hand, by bringing the future into the present, and, on the other hand, by bringing the past into the present. They made an abstract idealism actual and dynamic and a formal traditionalism instrumental. As was said, at the Crucifixion the Jew died, the Christian survived.

The Christian, however, survived as a subject of Rome. Still he was not a Roman, since both as Jewish money-lender and as Christian worshipper he was independent of Rome. His money and his Heaven were both superior to the restraints of pagan military Rome; and this superiority, as we know, Rome was very prompt to recognize, for the selfhood of Christ passed into her Imperator; whence Rome came to repeat in history the struggle and the sacrifice at Jerusalem.

But of Rome and her decline I shall speak in the following chapter. Let us take ship, then, as Paul did, and cross from Palestine, past the islands and peninsulas of Greece, to Italy and Rome.

---

[1] Or, as the same thing, *fulfilled* Judaism.

CHAPTER II.

ROME FALLS.

I.

ROME was a development, and she must illustrate a typical process; and just what the typical process is we ought to be able to determine from what we have seen of her dependence on Greece and Judea.

But this dependence suggests that the process of development is only the past getting into use, that is, becoming a perfected mechanism or tool for a revolutionary and evolutionary activity of the present. The Greek character and the Jewish character getting into use made Rome. Not that in these we have the only factors that entered into Roman life, but that they were certainly the most conspicuous factors, and afford an explanation of the fall as well as of the rise of the empire.

It is rather the common or conventional thing to say that Rome's rule was one of force, that her time was one when might alone made right or when physical forces were supreme, but to any such view we have to be altogether hostile. A time when might makes right is a time when a developed motive is at last free, or when an accomplished ideal is in full control, or when, to recall from above, the past is fully in use. Thus might made right, physical forces were operating, not less when you or I last took a walk to the post-office than when Rome's strength went abroad conquering the world. Because Socrates and Christ, in their different ways forestalled Rome, Socrates forestalling her rise and Christ forestalling her fall, Rome herself, only repeating their achievements, was as much will as force, right as might, opportunity as necessity, spirit as matter.

Socrates and Christ, furthermore, as men who liberated the past and thereby effected the free application of natural force and even in their individual lives anticipated great social movements, show just what genius is, and, as geniuses, they were related to the two chief incidents of Rome's activity, her rise and her fall. The one antecedently sanctioned, the other subsequently interpreted, Rome's imperialism. Of course sanction and interpretation are the two chief incidents of all activity; but it is not always recognized that decline and fall necessarily follow or even accompany interpretation.

Now, as to the first incident, the sanction, I

must here repeat a little from the chapters on Socrates. The antecedent conditions of Rome's imperial freedom were self-denial, and, as really only the other side of self-denial, a sense of universal selfhood. These, however, Socrates realized at his death, and through Stoicism, Epicureanism, and Scepticism they became real to all. Socrates' universal selfhood, moreover, was extremely abstract. It was the one; it was simply not any individual. But from the standpoint of such an abstraction and such a negation, we can see, as indeed we did see, how the imperial militarism arose. The individual, through self-denial made means or " measure " or brought into definite status, became at once an integral part of a political mechanism; and just in proportion as the negation, or the denial, was complete and as the scepticism was thoroughgoing, the mechanism was free to move. Indeed, from the standpoint of the parts, what better account could be given of a moving mechanism than that just suggested, action through self-denial and abstract unity of selves? Each part can be imagined to say, "I am not, because we are all one and equal." Certainly Socrates said that, and so sanctioned Rome.

But, furthermore, as to the other incident of activity, namely, the interpretation, this is first to be observed. The movement of a mechanism, particularly when its parts are sentient beings, when it is a social mechanism, — and I confess to wondering if any other kind of mechanism ever really moved, — is sure to start disintegration. The motion has the very natural effect of communicating to every part the selfhood, that is, the nature and motive and responsibility, of the whole, so that after motion has taken place every single part, from its own essentially different and peculiar standpoint, will feel, if it does not say, "I did it; mine was the action, mine the achievement." After the motion, in other words, will come individuality and competition. Thus before a battle what a mechanism an army is; afterwards, what a lot of ambitious individuals, each clamoring for special recognition, each imagining himself the agent of the whole! Yes, a sentient mechanism is a whole which upon action breaks into a group of microcosmic reproductions of itself; it is a whole whose self-expression produces a community of different selves, each and all acting in and with the original motive or ideal, but seeking at the same time individual independence, — in short, it is no sooner an acting moving mechanism than it becomes an organism.

Militarism, accordingly, brings into being, or rather reveals and makes ideal, social organism; and with the change the individual finds that his self-denial was self-expression, and that his unity with his fellows was really an organic unity. So, however true it be that Rome was not built in a day, it is equally true that she lived only for a day. Upon self-expression she outgrew herself; her division followed in the wake of her unification.

Hence in organism the movement of mechanism, that is, the activity of Rome, is interpreted. In it the conditions of militarism are made ideal, becoming only the recognized means to an already realized end or active motive. In the nature of organism, however, as he who runs may read, are the primal teachings of Christ, and in its activity are to be seen, free and living, the very forces or principles that Christ and his people liberated. Therefore, as was said, the activity that Socrates sanctioned, was subsequently interpreted by Christ.

II.

CAN there be found a more concise account of Christianity in its fulness than that in the simple word "organism"? In our day, certainly, no word is so rich in meaning, so truly the key of our modern life and thought. For what is truer of organism than that self-denial of the individual part is self-expression? Or what, than that reason ever belongs to the whole? Or, again, what than that responsibility is social? In responsibility as social, in this alone, lies all that is vital in the doctrines of incarnation, sacrifice, and resurrection. Organism, in fine, is the Christ-motive, — for that is what I like to call it, — which was liberated at the Crucifixion and which has survived on earth quite as truly as it has been said to have returned to Heaven. The course of history shows this.

Thus the course of history shows the decline of Roman imperialism before those two essentially Christian or Jewish principles, belief in a hereafter and interest in money here. Through the working of those principles organism, which was born at Christ's death or realized upon Rome's self-expression, has gradually thrown off its integument of mechanism.

And I feel now as if I hardly needed to enlarge upon the foregoing. I seem to myself to be getting dangerously near to the commonplace. Illustration, however, can do no harm, and even the commonplace is constantly getting a new meaning. So I may remind you, in the first place, that belief in an hereafter is evidence of organism succeeding mechanism, of social organism succeeding militarism, because it removes the basis of equality or unity among men wholly away from the life of worldly relations and places it in an wholly unworldly sphere. Socrates had taught an hereafter only negatively. Final reality, he had said, is not here and now; it is not ours; whither death leads no one knows, — perhaps to dreamless sleep, perhaps to some other world, where, as men say, all the dead abide; but Christ confidently taught, " In my father's house are many mansions." The difference is striking, and it is the difference between mechanism and organism in the life of men on earth. Does not heaven as an accomplished belief show the individual insisting upon some return for his services, upon some reward for his self-denial? Does it not show him claiming recognition of his own intrinsic worth, or asserting that within his own particular experience and as a part of his own deeper motive the life to which he belongs has justification, — that he is no slavish subject, but a responsible agent of that life? Belief in an hereafter saves the individual to himself at the same time that it relates him to all his fellows. True, he may need centuries in which to accomplish a freedom from all his chains, but with the belief his liberation begins.

But, in the second place, belief in an hereafter has had its counterpart, its earthly representative, in the interest in money here. Property as medium of exchange, abstract property, or money as coin, we found to be the unworldly in the world, it was Heaven's left hand; and quite as obviously as the hereafter it shows the assertion of individuality that the evolution of organism out of mechanism brought about. As medium of exchange money was an instrument of the organization or mutual adjustment of differences in interest or in occupation. In receiving it as a return for services, in giving it in payment of taxes, in use of it as the commodity in which all other commodities were one or in which all potentially resided, in regarding it as having value to the self only in possession or as serving immediately no vital function, no such function, for example, as that of satisfying hunger or affording shelter or pleasing the eye, in receiving it by inheritance or in willing it to others,[1] — in all these different ways the individual made unity or equality external to himself, but at the same time recognized a basis of an organic mutual adjustment among the members of the society to which he belonged.

Evidently the individual that was freed by the movement of the Roman mechanism became not only a religious creature by nature, but also a mercenary creature. He was both Christian and Jew. And, to venture upon an aphorism, it might be said that, if Socrates gave Rome her soldier-

---

[1] Inheritance of property, particularly of money, is by no means the least interesting way in which the Christian belief in an hereafter has had a worldly counterpart.

citizens,[1] Christ paid them. He paid them, through his people, with money; through himself, with a hereafter. Upon payment, however, they began to disband.

In selfish[2] sympathy or *instrumental* formalism we found a general term for both the Christian belief in the hereafter and the Jewish interest in money as representing the past or heretofore. Selfish sympathy was the belief or the interest in application as a social force, and we saw in it how Christendom was only repeating the conflict of her great teacher. Now, however, with more detail than before, let us turn to concrete history for illustration.

III.

ROME in action passed of necessity into Rome divided, — into Rome divided, however, in selfishly sympathetic parts, the division working down from larger to ever smaller parts, from nations towards individuals; and, as a result, from being pagan Rome became Christian. The process, however, had its important incidents as follows.

It brought, first, barbarian attack and invasion.

---

[1] That is, persons only by virtue of an assigned status, the *personæ* of Roman Law.

[2] Selfish, it ought to be said, not so much in original expression as to reflection or retrospection or subsequent interpretation.

Thus the conversion of Constantine, with its effect of making the whole empire Christian, heralded a rapid decline in the morality of Roman life by destroying or at least by greatly weakening the sense of responsibility to Roman institutions. Rome, like Greece in the days of Socrates, was brought into a face-to-face conflict with herself. But, whenever a people is in struggle with itself invasion is inevitable, being a perfectly natural part of the struggle. The weakness within invites attack from without; the strength within seeks expression without. Invasion indeed, it must be remembered, in political history as in individual experience, is only an attending circumstance of reversion, and progress is ever demanding reversion. Moreover, now to view the change more positively, the social organism that followed upon Rome's activity had been an altogether empty experience, if danger and final disaster, in perfectly visible form, had not come to Roman arms. Thus mechanism becoming organism, and paganism becoming Christianity, and the Roman arms finally even yielding to barbarian numbers were but one historical whole, or the related aspects of one historical movement. Development of the individual as member of a social organism at once increased his responsibilities, deepened his sense of the meaning of humanity, and made him in his own feelings ever less a Roman subject; and while out of his Roman eyes he was looking at his ever less Roman self and so preparing to welcome the Christian assurance of a soul and a heaven, the barbarians were swarming out of the north and the east, and it was as if they said: "Here in us is the opportunity of which you so abstractly dream. You are certainly no longer Romans. Then why try to be so? Why make reality a dream when you have it so close at hand?" In a sentence, Rome had outgrown herself, and, as at all times of outgrowing, so at that time nature did not fail to fulfil the larger destiny. In the swarming barbarians she provided force; she brought destruction; she created a stimulus answering to the developed motive; she helped a freed but backward will by making an apparent necessity.

But, secondly, Rome's division brought the separation of the Church from the State. The Roman Church, as representing the dream, had become a distinct institution before the fall. The removal of the capital to Constantinople had helped to bring this about by increasing the temporal power of the Bishop of Rome. In point of fact, so strong and so independent did the Church become, it was able to preserve both itself and the learning and the culture of the past, and with these eventually to overcome the victorious barbarians. The fall of imperial Rome was the rise of a still powerful ecclesiastical Rome. "The organization of the Latin State," we read,[1] "vitalized by a new spiritual force, vanquished the victors. It was the method and the discipline of this organization, not the subtlety of its doctrine, nor the power of its officials, that beat in detail one chief with his motley following after another. Hence, too, it came about that Christianity, which was adopted as the religion of Europe, was not modified to suit the various tastes of the tribes that embraced it, but was delivered to each as from a common fountain head." And again,[2] "when the surging tide of barbarian invasion swept over Europe, the Christian organization was almost the only institution of the past which survived the flood. It remained a visible monument of what had been, and by so remaining was, of itself, an antithesis of the present." Or, in terms repeated from above, it showed how a motive, developed in the past, was determined to apply to its own purposes the apparently blind forces of the present.

And, thirdly, closely connected with the separation of the Church was the rise of the bank as also a distinct social institution. Indeed, as so much

[1] J. Watt. The Latin Church: St. Giles' Lectures, 4th series.
[2] E. Hatch. The Organization of the Christian Church. p. 160.

has led us to think, the history of the Church in its relation to the State and the history of the bank belong together. Church and bank, as institutions in which Heaven, or the abstracted future, and money, or the abstracted past, were treasured or even hoarded, were naturally identified with the State, until division set in, since upon their abstractions imperialism depended. After division, however, their divorce from the State was inevitable, for their function, in the beginning imperial, naturally continued to be international. In them the original unity of the divided whole was preserved.

Nor was the separation of the bank from the State one whit less complete than we know that of the Church to have been. It did not, of course, come about all at once, but internationalism also took its time. The power of the Lombard and Florentine money-changers, however, and of the numerous banks of the Medici, and notably of the Bank of St. George at Genoa, shows how far the separation had gone in the Middle Ages. Of the last, the famous Bank of St. George, we learn[1] that it lived in complete independence of the government, "a state within a state, a republic within a republic," the "cradle of modern commerce, modern banking-schemes, and modern wealth,"

[1] See J. T. Bent's Genoa, ch. ii.

forming in "its constitution, its building, and its history, one of the most interesting relics of mediæval commercial activity." But its independence was incident to its natural international function, to its being the basis of unity in life among a number of extremely self-centred peoples. Like the Church at the time it was an agent of selfish sympathy; and this the more, as it was, although within a particular state, yet independent of the particular government.

As a matter of course, the Church and the bank were in the heat of the conflict to which they owed their origin. Thus the persistence of militarism made them both institutions in which the hereafter and the heretofore respectively were hoarded assiduously, while the new impulse, the Christ-motive, to an organic social life imposed a constant check upon the tendency to hoard. It had been Christ's part to bring Heaven down to earth, and to make his people use their accumulated experience. He made the future an actual motive and the past a substantial instrument. It was, then, the part of the Christ-motive that survived to do the same. Social organism, whether in international relations or in the separate lives of different peoples, required, on the one hand, that coin be brought into positive and direct earthly relations, becoming but one commodity among other commodities, and, on the other hand, that Heaven represent a future that could be defined in terms of actual conditions here and now. At just the moment, accordingly, when bank and Church had fully accomplished their separation from the State, the Reformation occurred, and capacity, or power, as the natural source of right to property and so a substantial basis of credit, was set up in protest against mere coin for medium of exchange; and justification by faith, against ecclesiasticism.[1]

But, finally, a fourth incident of Rome's division, and an incident very closely related to the foregoing, was the separation of the imperial monarch from distinctly earthly relations and responsibilities. The monarch became something of a figurehead, a large part of his original power being delegated to others. He became spiritualized, and with the change his dependence on money and Heaven for authority was made absolute. Other monarchs, rulers over parts of the original empire, rose into prominence, and were said for a time to have received their power from him; but their real sovereignty lay in the individual re-

---

[1] It here occurs to me that in passing I might suggest to those Germans who have wished to find a romance in social evolution, that the heroine in the case, as some have recognized, is the Church, while the hero must be no other than the bank. So at least can history be made biological.

sources of the particular peoples over whom they ruled, and the delegation of power came to be looked upon as a mere fiction. Yet, historically, it was not a mere fiction, since the imperialism was an antecedent condition of the internationalism. In the delegation of powers, too, in the spiritualization of the imperial ruler lay a natural check to monarchy and militarism. Plainly delegation implies limitation. Thus, from the standpoint of the spiritual ruler, who was, of course, the Pope, war among the parts of the empire seemed treachery, it seemed and indeed was wholly unnatural; and accordingly he held for a long period the place of peacemaker among the nations, he was the seat of international law. And from the standpoint of the several monarchs below him, war was unnatural also, for the simple reason that it was become wholly inconsistent with the basis of sovereignty. Hence militarism got its tendency towards armed neutrality, and monarchy, as Rome fell, became "limited." The Pope himself was, and still is, the "limited" monarch *par excellence*.

We often wonder how it happened that Rome's achievement was never repeated, but plainly there is no need of wonder. A military monarchy, merely upon expression of itself, creates its own natural check. A repetition of Rome was, therefore, absolutely impossible. Not only did the efforts at repetition fail signally, but also they had to fail. Simply, neither in Rome's time nor in later times, did might make right; or, to put the case in most general terms, after division had taken place, and we have seen that it had to take place, no resulting part could ever really will literally to repeat the life from which it had sprung. Impulse to repetition might exist, and in fact did exist, but not without some restraint from within as well as from without. No part could will to repeat the whole without doing the inconceivable, unnatural thing of willing to betray completely its own individuality. In short, the effect of the division was to throw each resulting part back upon its own peculiar characteristics and resources, back upon its own peculiar environment, for the natural sphere of its self-expression.

So, whether we view the course of history since the days of Rome from the standpoint of limited monarchy, or restrained militarism, or a divorced bank and church, whose hoarding even because of the divorce was checked, or of barbarian invasions,[1] we see how Rome came to her fall. Even like

---

[1] Of course *philosophically* the discovery and settlement of America was a barbarian invasion. In 1492, however, Rome had so far overcome herself that the invasion appeared rather as opportunity than as danger.

Christ, who had interpreted her to herself, she died for the sake of an organic social life.

IV.

But in still another way, and to me a very suggestive way, I would with a very few words show how Rome through her own self-expression came to decline and fall. In her spiritual monarchism, in her Jewish finance, in her jurisprudence, and in her literary formalism she did but fulfil and apply the Christian or Jewish idea of mediation.

Thus Christ, the fulfilment of Jewish life, as the World-Reason or the Word Incarnate, was God alive on earth, and the inner meaning of God living on earth was that the natural medium of man's self-expression, be it language, or political institutions, or coin, or a church, or what you like, was original or absolute or of intrinsic worth. *All* the different means, or media, of expression were made divine, and naturally at first the mediation seemed to be from another world. Hence the Roman theocracy with its reproduction of the city-state of the Greeks and its deified imperator. Hence, too, the idolatrous worship of Christ himself. Hence the scholasticism of the middle ages. Hence the imitating and copying and engrossing. Hence, finally, all the formalism for which Rome, spiritual and temporal, is known to-day, and from which, as Rome's natural heirs, we are not yet free, whether in our schools or our churches or our places of business or our social life generally.

But Christ and his people at the Crucifixion triumphed over Roman as well as over Jewish formalism. They showed that in originality or divinity of the medium of self-expression lay a complete refutation of formalism, not a justification of it. They demonstrated most emphatically, and history since their time has repeated the demonstration, that an original medium brings individual freedom, not individual subordination, — that it is a principle of the organization of differences, not of social conformity; and, in consequence, as we have seen, the other-world mediation, on which Rome was founded, changed with her decline to mediation in the conditions and the realities of the world here and now.

Briefly, the life of God on earth did not mean, and mankind has refused to understand it to mean, that the natural medium of self-expression is a dead language.

V.

FINALLY, the fatal interpretation of Rome's activity came to her not only in Christ, the prophet, but also in the art and the science and the philosophy that grew out of her repetition of his life, — defining it to her with increasing clearness and often with thoughtless cruelty, and in the end even betraying her altogether.

The great cathedrals and the great paintings and the great epics were Rome's attempts to naturalize, or acclimate, her supernatural authority. They were virtual arguments from the analogy of the supernatural to the natural, and they were as disastrous as such arguments always are. In them Rome sought to justify herself, but they only marked the sunset, golden and impressive, of her career. The Renaissance came with them.

And of the science I say only this. It was logic, interested merely in the abstracted medium of expression, in the Word Incarnate.[1] But, strange to say, although confining the reason to what seemed at the time an altogether appropriate and legitimate sphere, it found occasion to discuss, and in a timely way, the vital topic of the relation of part to whole, of individual to class or "universal." It was indifferent about the special phase of the mediation, spiritual or political, physical or literary, although from the nature of the case the literary had most attention. It simply concerned

---

[1] The Word Incarnate, as already implied, must be taken to refer to *all* the media of expression, not merely to written and spoken language; to Christ, to abstractly physical nature, etc.

itself with individuality, and moved in the direction that art was already taking. Thus it concluded that the unity of a group of individuals was not abstractly, or monarchically, or supernaturally determined,[1] and also, as complementary to this, that individuals were not in themselves naturally unrelated or without unity,[2] but that each individual *naturally* had in himself the supernatural "one" or "universal."[3] So long as this conclusion remained a doctrine of logic, so long as it was nothing but abstract or merely "physical" science, it was safe. A doctrine of logic, however, it ceased to be, so soon as it had been clearly stated; or at least, as a first step, it at once sanctioned an inductive science; and induction was fatal to the authority of Rome.[4]

But philosophy[5] followed logic as closely as logic had followed art, and the fatal interpretation was quickly brought to its natural limit. It is always the part of philosophy to carry to a limit whatever is assumed in an existing order of things. Thus, if you should imagine monarchy fully to realize its own ideal, the condition into which the

[1] As Realism had insisted.
[2] As the unwittingly sympathetic Nominalism insisted.
[3] Conceptualism.
[4] Of course logic became inductive as Rome's division approached its limit, the individual person.
[5] Metaphysics.

monarch and his subjects would come is exactly that which Spinoza defined as belonging to what, in his more general terms, he called Substance and its manifold modes. All that he said of substance, you would have to say of the monarch. You would find the monarch one, infinite, indivisible, self-existent or independent, self-intelligible or infallible, and you would give him as his essential attribute or prerogative a freedom of all limitations in space and time. And all that Spinoza said of the modes of substance, you would have to say of the subjects of the monarch. You would find them dependent upon each other only through the monarch himself; you would find them absolutely individual; you would find them not themselves substantial, but expressing the essential attributes of their substantial ruler. In short, you would conclude that Spinoza was saying, only in his philosopher's way, exactly what Louis XIV. at about the same time was both saying and enacting. "I am the state," Louis XIV. is reported to have said. But also you would see that a monarch, whether on the Bourbon's or on Spinoza's terms, would be a mere figure-head, a sheer abstraction for a condition, realized in the state, that must be quite inconsistent with subjection to any personal monarch. "I am the state," upon becoming true, would become also the most empty boast. It became that in history, did it not? I do not mean at once, but in course of time. Even Spinoza's monism was not appreciated at once. Rome controlled even the Jew Spinoza's mind.

Leibnitz, however, made one correction of Spinoza, and a correction that we are quite ready to applaud. Thus he said, in so many words, that on Spinoza's own terms individuals must be more than "modes" of a self-existent, self-intelligible substance; individuals must be independent self-active *forces*, the subjects of no monarch but monarchs all themselves, each with the same attribute, or prerogative, that Spinoza had given to his Substance. But this thought of Leibnitz is quite in line with what we saw some time ago, when we observed how political mechanism or imperialism upon fulfilment and expression of necessity communicated its own power and will and responsibility to each part acting in it. Only in Leibnitz's time the individual part was not the nation but the person, Rome's division having reached its limit. Leibnitz, however, although seeming to make the individual supreme, saved himself from being charged with a philosophy of anarchy. Like Spinoza, although in a different way, he remained loyal to the traditional order. He was not ahead of his times. In his doctrine of a pre-established harmony he paid his tribute to Rome, to whom tribute was still due.

And after Leibnitz came, Immanuel Kant, the last great Roman in philosophy, who, although making an important reservation, ascribed to the essential nature of the individual person all that Rome had assumed for her imperial self at the beginning. Indeed, it was as if he saw the subjects of Rome coming at last into their natural inheritance. Thus he declared, and I would dwell upon the words, that *space* and *time* [1] and *causation* [2] were natural endowments of the individual, not properties, or primary qualities, of the external world. But, and this was his reservation, he made them endowments of the mind, not of the soul; he made them forms or bases of knowledge, not forces or motives to action.[3] The heirs of Rome, accordingly, were free to observe or know, but not yet free to act; although intellectually free from the limitations of space and time and causation, they were not spiritually free in the world of their experiences; although become scientists, they still remained soldiers in Rome's army, and their life had still to look for mediation in another world.

[1] The attributes of Spinoza's Substance.
[2] Leibnitz's self-active force.
[3] Kant's reservation obviously had the same general purport as Leibnitz's doctrine of pre-established harmony.

But they were like soldiers without the needed leader, in whom the other world could reveal itself. The very freedom that had been given them had taken their leader from before their eyes; or, if with a leader, they could not hear his orders, nor know his purposes, nor in any way relate themselves to the sphere of his interest and activity. They might know knowledge; they might blindly do deeds, acting from no other motive whatsoever but that of duty, the habit of loyalty still controlling them; they might turn slavish officials; but the service of a leader, whom they could see, was once for all denied them. The Word, it is true, was left; but the Word Incarnate, as at the time of Christ's death, so now at the time of Rome's death, had gone whence it was said to have come.

And if we have never wondered that Judas killed himself, we certainly cannot wonder that in Kant's time there were those who, finding nothing to know but an idea and nothing to do but a deed, concluded, although quite in a doctrinal way, that suicide was the only means to complete self-realization. Had not Rome's division reached the individual person? And has the individual Roman, has the soldier, anything but death to look forward to? Should he not, then, as if with a consummate heroism, bring death upon himself?

No, said Kant; for never by his own will could the individual deny his loyalty to the Word. The individual could never do anything but loyal deeds, and his suicide would be distinctly disloyal, since it would bring him to a denial both of himself and of the whole to which he belonged. As a suicide, in short, he would have to do the impossible thing of becoming traitor to the motive of his own act. Or, to make Kant's reasoning quite concrete and historically real, while it may be true that death is the soldier's natural goal, yet this is very far from meaning that death is also his natural motive. Were it to become his motive, he would cease to be the soldier that he was, and so would have it no longer as his natural goal; or, were he able to take his own life, he would no longer have the reason for doing so. At the very moment of action, should he arrive at it, dark though his life might seem, he would find himself more than the soldier of an unseen leader, he would find himself self-active, an independent agent, the master at least of the tool of his own destruction, his own leader; he would come at last into his complete inheritance, the Word rising again in the life of its still loyal servant.

And Kant, accordingly, as if in view of this promise, gave to his individual another selfhood than that of the soldier-scientist, and to the world another reality than that of a possible object of mere knowledge. He said, it is true, that the individual's other selfhood and the world's other reality were unknowable; but at his time and from his standpoint, Roman that he was, he could have said nothing else. His teaching, however, meant, alike in its own inner logic, and in the history which it has reflected so accurately, that knowledge, *whenever put into application*, brings its possessor into a substantial independence of its mere forms, or that, as we saw before, the soldier in action ceases to be a soldier.

So was Kant not only the philosopher of Rome's downfall, the last great Roman philosopher, but also the herald of a new life that was to come. With the dogmatism of a prophet, a dogmatism that in him, as in others, has been too often criticised, he declared that faith still had an object. He was loyal to the past; but so fully did he define it that the future, of which the people had long been dreaming, was shown to be at the hour of its realization. The downfall of Rome, like the death of Christ, was not occasion for despair.

Part III.

RESURRECTION.

THE CHRISTIAN STATE.

I.

HOW far this third part of the present study is necessary I cannot determine, but drawing conclusions always seems so idle and so uncomplimentary. If it does not cast unwelcome reflections upon the reader, it certainly does cast them upon the writer. It is quite like the child's way of naïvely labelling his imperfect picture; or, with special regard to the interest here, it is as if, like the doubting Thomas, one could not see with one's own eyes what had become already present and visible. And yet, true as this is, I face the accusation that will be cast upon me and ask my question: What is it that we see? But I remember, perhaps with a little comfort, that although Rome's fall was years ago, the people of the world about me have not yet ceased to stare in vacancy and wonder. They, too, have been asking: What is it that we see?

What we and they have seen is the simple process of Rome's division. Doubtless Carlyle, with his senses so much more awake to all the incidents, would have called it rot or decomposition. But, names aside, we have seen, as intimately related to Rome's decline, the limitation of monarchy, the growing dependence of different peoples upon their natural resources, the widening of the Roman or Christian-Jewish influence, and the rise of a would-be militant and imperial finance and of a not less tyrannical ecclesiasticism.[1] Other incidents there were also, such as loss of patriotism and rise of moral irresponsibility, and such as art, science, and philosophy; but we found that we could bring them all under one formula, discovering in them all evidence of a progressive abstraction, or "translation," of the medium of expression, and with the help of one of the philosophers we saw that this abstraction reached its completion so soon as the division had found a limit in the individual person. The Medium, the leader, the Incarnate One, was at the last shown to be as unknowable as he had been infallible.[2] Language became dead.

[1] Even Protestantism, it must be remembered, as opposed to Romanism, has been only a reactionary ecclesiasticism. It has not yet brought an essentially different Christianity.

[2] Of course this change is illustrated in the Papacy losing

But the fatal conclusion of the process was significant, because it brought to the hour of its birth, in the individual persons of the empire, the motive and activity that had originally been communalistic or imperial, and, as has been intimated already, this closing chapter is added only to show beyond all possibility of doubt the reality of the new birth. To any, who will examine its marks, the individualism of our own time is Rome risen again; in it the Word has been fulfilled in a resurrection.

II.

BUT recall how we were able to say, as if in sympathy with his subjects, that the Roman emperor was God alive on earth, and how we discovered the closest connection between the decay of imperial monarchy and the decline of militarism. The connection, moreover, was an evidence to us of the reality of the Christ-motive, or of the impulse to organism, trying to free itself from social mechanicalism. But one phase of the process, perhaps the most significant of all, has so

its temporal power, virtually a century ago, although nominally as recently as 1870, when Rome became the capital of the Kingdom of Italy. For the decline of the Pope's power in the eighteenth century see Pennington's " Epochs of the Papacy," ch. x.

far escaped our notice, although throughout it has been before our eyes.

To monarchy has belonged a peculiarly Christian function. Whether we look to the Roman emperor or to the monarchical ruler over smaller dominion, we see in the monarch the tendency to become a mediator in the very special sense which religion has given to the name. Thus, although naturally at the head of the army, he is in all other political offices of ever lessening importance, and so appears as one who assumes his people's outgrown past, namely, their militarism, and by drawing off so much of their political sinfulness accomplishes their political salvation. And history, be it said also, in order to show how complete the obvious analogy may become, has demonstrated more than once that his death, instead of merely his partial limitation, may be necessary for a complete realization of a people's freedom from its sinful past. Why, Thomas Hobbes, theorizing about the state and its origin, and trying to give a philosophical justification of the claims of the Stuarts, unwittingly showed the monarch in just this light. He made the monarch the personal agent of the people by contract, and the monarch is the agent of the people, but by nature, not by mere contract, and of so much of the people's activity as they are outgrowing, not of the activity newly arisen among them; he stands for what they are ceasing to be, not for what they are becoming.

How morally corrupt a monarch and his court become, as the check upon militarism asserts itself! To the new life he and it feel ever less responsibility. The duty that his people recognize he and it cannot know. Such is his position that lawlessness is impossible to him; he cannot transgress. In his life, then, one sees repeated, although rather as so much natural process than as the responsible action of an individual's will, the career and the achievement of Christ.

But, says some one, such a repetition of Christ's achievement in the monarch's life is the merest fancy, founded on some unwarrantable metaphor. Yet it is no fancy; it is no metaphor. Was not Christ's death a signal triumph over militarism and all its incidents? And the Christian doctrine of salvation, what is it but peculiarly of salvation from the sins of war? In the Pope, too, the function of Christian mediation, belonging to the military monarch, has had a very positive expression. Not, however, until one has followed the mediating process from the papal apex of the feudal pyramid to the populous base can one adequately measure the vitality of the Christ-motive at work in it.

The feudal pyramid is so much more a history of Europe than a monument of any particular time. It is so much more a force than a formal condition. We may not wonder that the ordinary observer fails to see the molecular movements and the dynamic character in general in the material object, but how historians have been so often blind to the living process in feudalism is hard to understand. No man can really watch the pyramid attentively without seeing in it an upward and a downward movement, the effect of which, in fact, is to make it more sphere than pyramid, and which in itself is none other than the double movement of history. For is it not plain? As with the successive divisions and the progressive delegations and limitations of power the base itself at last becomes, so to speak, a manifold of apexes, as the people at large finally become monarchs, but limited monarchs of course, the pope becomes nothing but a spiritual figure-head. Simply, the process is one in which the principle of monarchy is gradually secularized or popularized — this being the downward movement — and the monarch himself is gradually spiritualized — this being the upward movement, and we do not need Heraclitus to tell us that the way up and the way down are the same. We know, however, that monarchy brought to the base of the pyramid, or the monarch made figure-head, is democracy, and we have to conclude that in democracy, if adjudged from its origin, all being monarchs, all must be also living expressions of the Christ-motive. Feudalism, in fine, as dynamic, as a process instead of a condition, means nothing less than this. In it, from the beginning, there was the certainty of the liberation of the individual.

In a word, democracy is the inevitable goal of monarchy; not, however, in any fatal way, but in fulfilment of an inner motive; and in democracy the individuals are still Romans, since each will have imperial rights over some single line of activity, and will in this be the saving monarch of all the others. Have we not seen how the action of a political mechanism not only divides the original whole, but also creates differences among the parts? The differences, however, are not by nature in conflict; rather are they the related phases of one life; so that the different parts expressing them must act, one and all, in the interests of the whole. " Division of labor" the process is often called, but men have not usually noticed just how division of labor was made possible, nor how it liberates, in the mutual relations of the separate laborers, the essentially Christian functions of incarnation, resurrection, and salvation.

You fail to catch my meaning? I seem to be

using most sacred words idly and even irreverently? In my understanding of the evolution of democracy from monarchy you cannot allow me even the idea of an inheritance of mere functions? But I ask you only to consider how the assumption of any special phase of a society's activity must make the individual assuming it the mediator and savior of society in respect to just so much of the social life. Indeed, my notion is this, that just so far as an individual expresses his own individual selfhood he is without sin himself, but has at the same time taken upon himself what for all others of his kind has become sinful. Surely it is the natural right of each individual to express himself, and also no two individuals are alike. All, however, are mutually dependent, else their individuality would be without meaning. The free expression of any one, then, brings redemption to all the others; or, to cap these commonplaces, society is an organism whose own freedom of action depends on the integrity of that of its separate members.

We talk of the conflict of good and evil, but we might call it the conflict of democracy and monarchy. The criminal is by nature a monarchical leader, revealing the sins of those who condemn him; and his judges, at the moment of his crime, are but so many soldiers marshalled in his cause. Only remember that it is as much the indifference of others as the interest of the offender that makes a crime possible. He is the will, but they are the force. Was it not indifference that made Rome's activity possible and that brought the birth of Christ? Society, moreover, in one way or in another way, always crucifies the criminal in whom it sees itself condemned. The two thieves, on the right hand and on the left hand of Christ, belonged there.

And if the criminal is by nature a monarch, the monarch is also by nature a criminal.[1] This, in fact, we have seen already. But, I say again, changing my words, that the monarchical or individual leadership of others must ever bring lawlessness upon the leader, and lawfulness upon them that follow. Thus the political "boss" leads on such terms; and so, too, the money-king. Licentious gods, also, have saved their worshippers.

So, obviously, to conclude this analysis, crime with all the evil that attends it is an incident of social evolution as useful as it is painful. It accompanies the decomposition that turns mechanism into organism. It is the past rising in condemnation of the thoughtless conventionalism of the present. It is, finally, monarchy through the

[1] Or law-breaker. It would be interesting, from the standpoint here taken, to study the history of Jurisprudence.

vitality of the Christ-motive passing into its new life, democracy.[1]

III.

BUT the individuals of the modern democracy must be Romans also. As is said above, each one must have imperial rights over some single line of activity. Yet just how can this be? Plainly, only through the invention and use of machinery. The Roman, you remember, at the moment of possible suicide found himself no longer a soldier, but a person with a tool in his hand, and the will to use it, but not on himself. The tool, of course, revealed to him a new way of gaining the wished-for independence of the limitations of space and time. If, then, monarchy has risen again in democracy, militarism has had its resurrection in industrialism or the commercial use of machinery.

Industrialism, however, is nothing new in itself, although its birth in the individual person is comparatively new. Industrialism began, at least for what we know as the Christian era, at the very

---

[1] How unintentionally keen the lawless author of the "Fable of the Bees" was!

Thus of society: "Every part was full of vice
        Yet the whole mass a paradise."

And again: "Such were the blessings of that state,
        Their crimes conspired to make them great."

moment when the division of Rome began. At the moment of division the resulting parts, as we have found, were thrown back upon their individual natural resources for their appropriate spheres of self-expression, and this only means that they were made to face the necessity of realizing their Roman selfhood, or of repeating their Roman activity, in the narrower confines of individual environments.

Now, I am neither mathematician nor economist, but one hardly needs to be anything, except an observer, to see that with such necessity would come the mechanicalization of those individual environments. The former militarism would be inhibited, but only that the freedom in space and in time which it had effected, might be adapted to the new conditions. Adaptation, however, would obviously bring the invention and use of machinery and consequently the rise of industrialism. True, industrialism began with agriculture; but simply because division began with nations and classes. Certainly it was an agriculture in which the land came to be used scientifically or mechanically. The early system of rents and the condition of the toilers are evidence of that. Again, I know that it was a form of industrialism whose commerce among the parts was rather through strife and lawlessness than through any clearly intended co-operation; but the motive to free exchange and organization was not wanting. Only as the division worked down to its limit could the motive to commerce expect to be finally free. The liberation of the individual and the free application of his independence of space and time could not come all at once.

We have seen that the Greek mathematician reached the conception of the atom, or infinitesimal indivisible unit, at the same time that Socrates came into the conviction of an unworldly, or spaceless and timeless and immaterial hereafter, and also that, so long as the conception and the conviction were only negative, they were sanctions of Rome's political mechanicalism. Christ, however, and his people made them positive, turning them into motives or principles of self-expression instead of the mere principles of self-denial that paganism had found them, so that it was by no strange coincidence that a life controlled largely by the longing for heaven, and a science of mechanics which applied the infinitesimal, not as a composite part, but as a mechanical force, to physical phenomena, developed together.[1] But the application, I repeat, brought

---

[1] Certainly to see this intimate connection between the longing for heaven and the dynamics of the infinitesimal is to conclude that, whatever may be said of theology, science and religion have not

industrialism, and with it the resurrection of Rome's armies. Industrialism has had, naturally enough, its own incidents; for example, the post, the press, the telegraph, the engine, the factory, and all the various means of communication and transportation and commercial manufacture; but, one and all, from early times to the present day, they show mechanical force in use, and in use with the natural[1] result, that social life the world over has been made ever less dependent on conditions of mere time and mere distance, and that the individual has come ever nearer to securing imperial power even in the expression of his own individual selfhood.

Now do we see, perhaps more clearly than before, what Kant meant when he allowed to the individual no inheritance but that of the principles of space, time, and causality. Those principles show Kant's way of reporting the power to use mechanical force that the individual had gained from his past; and Kant's "thing-in-itself," the world in its ultimate reality, was the world as a

---

been so much in conflict as has been commonly supposed. In heaven man has hoped for a freedom from this world's limitations, and in the infinitesimal, not less spaceless and timeless than heaven itself, he seems to be nearing, if not to have won, what he hoped for.

[1] "Natural," because the effect was already in the cause. The infinitesimal, as abstraction for mechanical force, contains in itself the freedom of space and time limitations.

perfectly free mechanism,[1] which the individual was absolutely free to use. But Kant, the Roman, checked the freedom, as if it were after all only theoretically real, enjoining rather the life of the keen observer, the soldier-scientist, than the life of the revolutionist. Revolution came, however, and violently in some quarters, although nowhere without some evidence of evolution. The activity had to come, since the philosopher could do no more than accurately define the conditions upon which it was to take place. He might define the force, but he could not destroy it. He might bid men look before they leaped, but he could not stop their leaping. Was not the mechanism usable? And was not the activity as old as Rome herself? And the activity, the use, as it came, brought the death of the soldier and the birth of the mechanic, in whom — so we are able to say here — there resided the certain promise of both an imperial power and a substantial Christian responsibility.

[1] Of course the *noumenon*, which was "unknowable" only in so far as not used; but, when used, spaceless and timeless. Pure mechanics has the Kantian *noumenon* in the particle as an atom of force moving in the infinitesimal time-interval over the infinitesimal distance.

IV.

BUT a democracy, a Christian state, has among its institutions a bank and a church; and to these, in view of all that has been said above, we must give special attention.

Of the present time, in which democracy is so distinctly the vital ideal,[1] it may be said that a large part of the Bank's legitimate business is carried on outside of the Bank itself, — for example, by the express companies, by the telegraph companies, by such publications as Bradstreet's and Dun's, by the various trade-journals, and even by the newspapers. So true is this that one has no choice but to conclude, in terms which should by this time have a meaning here, that banking has risen, the stone having been rolled away, even while its mere devotees were worshipping at the sepulchre.

Yet what is the Bank's legitimate business? Well, aside from the heretical agencies of banking just referred to, it seems to me that in the growing futility of hoarding,[2] in the lowering rate of inter-

---

[1] Witness the conflict of those complementary opposites, unsocial individualism and un-individualistic socialism or communalism.

[2] Hoarding has always been met by a demand for fiat-money; but this is only the reaction, and in itself can hardly be said to have checked the evil. The interaction, however, of the dogma of

est, and, above all else, in the increasing use of credit-instruments,[1] such as checks, notes, bills of exchange, and the like, we have an evidence, which is even final, that the Bank's real business is to make commercial intercourse possible for all members of society without the necessity either of personal intercourse or of transportation of coin. Is any other conclusion possible? Is the assumption by the Bank of any other function than this desirable?

What it all means, of course, is that in the Christian state, in which the individual is to be a Christian through having imperial rights over a

hoarding and the fiat-heresy, has brought the real check. Thus, although the banks have hoarded coin or specie, and to-day probably more persistently than ever before, yet their hoarding has lost or is fast losing its military power, credit succeeding specie as the medium of exchange. The Incarnate Medium, whether silver or gold, is dead (or at least on its death-bed).

[1] The last report of the Comptroller of the Treasury specially recommended laws to encourage the issue of credit-instruments. Also two illuminating incidents in the history of German banking happen to come to my notice even as I am writing. The first is the rise of the group of land-credit and land-mortgage banks at the time of the seven years' war, and the subsequent extension of the system to the cities, with great benefit to the agricultural classes and to the population at large. The second is the curious use that has been made by the Germans of a large part of the famous French indemnity fund. Thus they have laid it away, *for use in case of war*, but have also put it into circulation through an issue of notes not necessarily redeemable. Both of these cases show the relation of militarism to the currency, and the change that peace demands.

single individual activity, namely, over his own complete self-expression, no other medium of exchange is possible than that of credit, of inalienable, unquestionable, substantial, dynamic credit. But what would be the source of such credit? Exactly that which is its source now, the mechanic's power to apply the world's force. And what would make such credit a possible medium? Exactly what makes it a medium now, the power of accurate and prompt information or intelligence the world over. Let the Bank be what in so many ways, although quite as much without as within its visible self, it already is, an institution, not for the keeping of treasure, but for exchange through credit.[1] Let it be an institution through

---

[1] Of course it is obvious enough, as so many economists insist, that credit cannot be an absolute, or generally used, medium except on a perfectly free international basis. Thus, under international bimetallism, coin would cease to be the medium; credit would have to take its place. Bimetallism marks a process, not a condition, and the end of the process is credit. International bimetallism, in other words, would make the visible medium not even dual but as manifold as the commodities to be exchanged. And I sometimes wonder, as I reflect upon the part that the Chinese finances took in our recent campaign, and as I at the same time look hesitatingly into the future, if it may not be in the further evolution of human society the part of the still uncivilized or only partially civilized oriental peoples to set credit finally free in commercial life. At least, when credit is free, I should look for their admission into a perfectly free and correspondingly worldwide commercialism. Certainly they have been at least one degree more traditional, more conventional, more credulous,

which any individual part of society can know, with the promptness and the confidence that action demands, exactly what capacity for action belongs to all other individual parts.¹ Let it be a thoroughly useful social institution, not an institution that is useful only to a particular class, and that marshals others into an army of mere ser-

than the Jews were, and at the proper time might be expected to bring the past, in their consciousness so much more remote, so much longer cherished, so much more completely defined and organized, into the actual use of mankind the world over.

[1] The social organism, it is frequently said in these times, is not analogous to the individual organism, at least in respect to the seat of its consciousness. Society, the contention is, has no central consciousness, no single will. Yet political philosophy and psychology have always been most curiously parallel. Along with spiritual monarchy there has been a spiritual, monarchical psychology, first expressing itself in logical terms (cf. the abstract idea or concept), then later, upon the protestant reaction, in physiological terms (cf. the brain as monarch of the body). Psychology has had its feudalism too, its doctrines of association by contiguity and abstract similarity and arbitrary classification, and of "idea-centres" and arbitrary "reactions." And, not to make the story too long, psychology is saying to-day with great clearness that the soul, or self, is not a resident of the body to which some special locality can be assigned, but a principle, a function of the body's activity; *and, as to consciousness, this rather identifies itself with the particular organ in action than adheres to any arbitrarily selected part.* Of course the idea of organism has made such a psychology possible. Moreover, if society is found to be an organism, I know no reason why, upon the discovery, the idea of organism should not become in itself an organizing idea. If society is an organism, then the organism is not exactly what hitherto it has been supposed to be. The analogy, then, may not hold, but that is not society's fault, nor the fault of any form of *reality*.

vants. The Bank should make it possible for skilled labor to find a market.

I have called credit dynamic, and you must see why it is dynamic. It sanctions the movement of machinery; in the popular phrase, it "turns the wheels of industry." Indeed credit, as such a thinker as Spinoza would be likely to say, is only an attribute of the real substance of industrial life, the other important attribute being machinery. For the substance, however, society has a name. Thus credit and machinery are the two inseparable attributes of the substance "capital." Credit is capital on the side of mind; machinery, on the side of matter. Moreover the common definition of capital as wealth in actual use or expression, or as productive wealth, is quite in accord with this Spinozistic account; and perhaps no conclusion of the whole analysis is more striking than this, that in the Christian state labor and capital cannot represent two classes, but one. Make credit the basis of exchange, and you will find no laborer that is not also a capitalist and no capitalist that is not also a laborer. The individual in the Christian state is not an owner of mere wealth on the one hand, nor yet on the other an owner of mere bodily force; he is self-active, having in himself both wealth and force; he is a mechanic, a skilled laborer.

Now, a moment ago, I said that the Bank should make it possible for skilled labor to find a market, and doubtless I seemed to be asking what might in many cases be quite impossible; but the simple fact is that through its very origin skilled labor must always have some exchange value. Its value, it is true, must be measured by the social demand, but the social demand will be proportional to the integrity of the laborer's individual self-expression. The important fact, however, is that individuality has a natural value in exchange, and that in consequence to ask the Bank to find a market for it is not to ask an impossibility. But, you say, it is to ask what is only theoretically possible, and I answer that nothing is quite so practical as a theory that defines what has been done and is being done every day in the year. Such a theory only urges mankind to do more thoroughly, more comprehensively, more vitally, what it always has been doing. Let the Bank, then, do for the individual in the remotest villages and in the humblest stations what it now is doing for the more favored classes in the towns and cities.[1] In short, let it do its part toward making a free individualism successor to the competitive

[1] Our cities with their congested life are largely the result of money the medium, instead of credit; of imperfect communication and uncertain transportation. "Postal banks" are a movement in the right direction.

individualism, from which *even* to-day we are suffering.

Three aspects of one thing, — that is in fact what we have now before us: first, a free individualism; second, a freely moving mechanism;[1] and, third, a credit-bank. And of the second of these I would add that in it, in machinery, exactly the same essential function is served as that which language serves. Indeed written and spoken language is but a part of the complete mechanism of expression. Some, I know, have thought of language as the basis of an absolutely common life among individuals, as the mere medium of the exchange of abstract thought; but certainly language is not that. Language is a great deal more. It is a medium of individuation or of social organization or of the mutual adjustments of individuals. It is a basis of a socially organic activity. The mediæval logicians did well to identify it with Christ, the Word; but since their time man has found himself individually self-active in other ways than the ways merely of reading and speaking and writing.[2]

---

[1] Of transportation, communication, and manufacture.

[2] This tempts me to speak of the resurrected school, but upon it I think I can leave any possible reader to think for himself. In regard to the larger idea of language, here suggested, I venture to refer to an article of my own on "The Stages of Knowledge," in the *Psychological Review* for January, 1897.

And the thought to which I would here give expression is a large one, and I know not how to state it adequately to myself. It brings such extremes together. It shows how, underlying the change from natural force as applied through the movement of armies to natural force as applied through such great instruments of social expression and individual redemption as the engine and the press and the telegraph, there is only a motive, original in man's life, realizing itself. If you have followed and understood, you have seen how it Christianizes or spiritualizes the most material conditions of life, and, more than all, how it materializes, that is, how it makes positively and actually real on earth, real and so possible, the Christian life, freeing the Christian impulse, making Christianity anything but a mere sentiment. Still how can I express it? I have found, as you see, no better account than this. It is resurrection.

V.

BUT to the Church a resurrection also. Exactly what was said here of the Bank has been said again and again of the Church of to-day. A large part of its legitimate business is carried on outside its walls. But who can wonder? Have not democracy and free industrialism, material conditions though they are, been the means of liberating the Christ-motive? Democracy and industrialism are saying to Christian people with an emphasis never before so strong, "Now is the accepted time; now is the day of salvation." In realizing the Christ-function in every individual, they call for a freer, more positive expression of Christianity. What the Christian is, they seem to say, what he is, as it were in spite of himself, just that the Christian ought to be. Thus, in the sense which I have tried to give the term, the mechanic is by nature a Christian. Then the Christian ought to be a mechanic wholly responsible to the use of his realized opportunity. So, again, who can wonder that Christianity has left its church, in which the military worship or hoarding of the future is still continued?

Under the Empire it was natural that Christianity should be before all else a separate church, and only the more as the Empire declined, just as it was natural that the other world should be life's chief motive, and that men should be soldiers, and that money as mere coin should be the medium of exchange; and under limited monarchy, as the separation widened, it was natural that Christianity should be sectarian, just as it was natural that there should be standing armies and competitive individualism in general; but under a real democracy and a free industrialism there must be, in place of a separate church and in place of sects, a free Christianity. With the change from monarchy to democracy, from a society of soldiers to a society of laborers, from coin and armies to credit and machinery, there must come a change in religion from worship and sentiment to far-seeing effective practice or truly mediated Christian activity, in short from faith to realization.

The Church has this great lesson to learn from history. Division, or decomposition, is not death. The Christ-motive, so vital, so persistent in human experience since the Crucifixion, has only repeated its great prophet's triumph. Decomposition is not death, but immortality; it is the soul struggling toward free expression; it is the life of undying organism. Matter is not composite, but organic. After decomposition, then, resurrection.

Yes, this is plainly the Church's lesson from history; and, although it was set so long ago, history was necessary before it could be learned.[1] Now, however, that it has been learned, the Church's interest in the salvation of men's souls must turn, and has already turned, into the interest in their more vital expression. Briefly, the soul

---

[1] What an evidence of this necessity we have in the "Higher Criticism"! Christianity has been so obviously the product of *retrospective* interpretation.

as organism is neither mortal nor immaterial, but both immortal and material; and neither original sin nor original perfection can be ascribed to it, since in neither way is it without substantial responsibility. Expression, then, is man's single duty to it, and expression is possible here and now, because already made manifest in history.

Salvation, however, as already realized in the soul's expression here and now, or the more vital expression of his living self as man's *religious* duty, must affect the Church in two important details: first, in respect to its prayer, and second, in respect to its ritual. Is not the Word, in which the individual can express himself, the whole world of his experience? And is not the individual become free, or self-active, in the wholeness of his selfhood? Once, it is true, only eyes and ears were freely his, but now all things are his. His prayer, then, and his ritual should change accordingly.

In the resurrected Church, evidently, the only prayer to which an answer can come, or which can be offered with a real religious faith, is such a consciousness as shall define to oneself all the conditions of one's life. Real prayer must be the earnest, honest, trusting definition of the sphere of one's activity; it must be the completest possible knowledge becoming motive. Indeed, I think, prayer always has been this, and is this now. Anything else is not prayer. But in modern science lies the completest possible knowledge of the whole self's sphere of action. Then it falls to the Church, the institution in which men pray, to turn science into motive. Why, what can prayer be but mind liberating the soul?

But you bid me remember that prayer must be addressed to some personal being. So it must, and the prayer of mind, which is the only prayer that the actual Christian can ever offer, is so addressed. It is addressed to the larger life, to the life in which one "lives and moves and has his being;" and by as much as man himself is personal, by at least so much is the life to which he belongs and to which he prays personal too. Must not the answer to prayer always be an act, an act of adjustment, an act in which an inclusive life is set free in an included part, an act which brings the part into a more vital assertion of itself? But such an act, bringing its agent into communion with the life including him, is proof that the prayer had been addressed to a personal being. The history that we have been studying is proof of the efficacy of prayer. "Father, forgive them; for they know not what they do." God ever is what those who pray do.

And, if science becoming motive or mind liberating the soul is the natural prayer of the resurrected Church, then its ritual must plainly be the action that this frees, or service of the God to whom the soul so liberated belongs. Such service, however, or such action, is the life of the present, and only in a church with this ritual can the Christian mechanic, citizen as he is of a redeeming democracy, feel at home. Indeed, as prayer is mind liberating soul, ritual is body expressing it.

The Church to-day cannot hoard the future, for the future is now and is open to all. It cannot make the life of the soul a protected industry, an industry by itself, for the soul is actual in all life. It cannot be divided by creeds, for its responsibility is to the lives of its members. It cannot seek members, for all men already belong to it. And it cannot be founded on a mere sentiment for unity, for it is itself unity.

Then what can it do? It can do exactly what it is doing, but more freely, more earnestly, more completely, with more of the self-denial that it has so long enjoined. It can identify itself with the Christ-motive that lives in society to-day. " Inasmuch as. ye have done it unto one of these, my brethren, even these least, ye have done it unto me." The Church is no longer the four steepled walls, that it has been so long, nor the altar, about which men have gathered and sought security in the hereafter, nor even the person Christ, who lived and taught at Jerusalem and finally returned to the Father; it is, above all else, a life that is responsible to conditions here and now.

In fine, in the course of history, State and Church are again one. Then an invisible Church? Yes, to him that still tarries at the lifeless tomb of walls and creeds, but not to him that goes among men, not to the citizen.

VI.

SOCRATES, in whom Greek anticipated Roman in the conquest of Greece, sanctioned militarism and monarchism. Christ at his death interpreted to itself the activity that Socrates sanctioned. And, as a result of the interpretation, organism began its struggle for liberation from the shackles of mechanism; and this struggle, beginning so long ago and continuing to the present day, has been a repetition in the life of human society of the career of Christ, a repetition of his struggle and a repetition of his death.

And, in our own day, the rising again.

THE END.

www.ingramcontent.com/pod-product-compliance
Lightning Source LLC
Chambersburg PA
CBHW030352170426
43202CB00010B/1351